Berlitz®

Nile Cruising

Front cover: a view of the Nile at Aswan

Right: temple statue at Dakkah, Lake Nasser

TOP 10 ATTRACTIONS

Abu Simbel • Rameses II's temples reflected the glory of Egypt and his reign, and deterred attackers from the south *(page 59)*

Philae Temple • Take a boa to this beautiful island temple surrounded by the waters of the Nile *(page 39*

Colossi of Memnon • These two statues are dazzling in their size *(page 78)*

Valley of the Kings • See the tombs of the great pharaohs, including the Tom of Tutankhamun *(page 72)*

fu Temple • Egypt's best-preserved temple *(page 34)*

Nubia Museum • Reveals the ancient land hidden beneath Lake Nasser *(page 49)*

eat Hypostyle Hall, rnak • These massive lumns embody the might Ancient Egypt *(page 64)*

Jabal As Silsilah • Behold carvings, temples and quarries along the Nile between Edfu and Kom Umbo *(page 36)*

xor Temple at night • e the majestic site beau- illy illuminated *(page 66)*

***Felucca* sailing** • Skim across the Nile on a traditional sailing boat to the West Bank at Luxor, or around the islands at Aswan – ideally at sunset *(page 62)*

A PERFECT DAY

5.30am Balloon flight

An early start for a stunning sunrise balloon flight over the West Bank at Luxor. Silently float over villages, fields and ancient sites whilst looking across the Nile or Hatshepsut's Temple, brilliantly illuminated by the morning rays.

7.30am Breakfast

Stay on the West Bank for an energising breakfast of *fuul* beans scooped up with discs of local bread and steaming hot tea. Try one of the roadside restaurants near the ferry terminal.

8.30am West Bank

Hire a bicycle to ride past the Colossi of Memnon and visit Dayr Al Madinah. Inside this ancient workmen's village is the superb tomb of Sennedjem, a painter who decorated Royal Tombs in the Valley of the Kings. Return via Medinat Habu, the funerary temple of Rameses III.

11.00am Go shopping

Catch a ferry across the Nile to the East Bank at Luxor and wander the alleys of the souq and the tourist shops. Bargain for statues, silks, jewellery, cotton, leather and metalware.

1.00pm Lunch

Several hotels have lunchtime restaurants with views of the Nile. For more activity, try one of the smaller restaurants overlooking the small but bustling souq just behind Luxor Temple, such as the Jamboree Restaurant (tel: 012-781 3149), serving Egyptian and Western fare.

IN LUXOR

2.00pm Pool and tea

Relax by the pool of one of the luxury hotels, most of which offer day passes for non-residents. Later on, afternoon tea at the prestigious Nile Terrace Café in front of the Winter Palace Hotel is always a pleasure.

5.00pm *Felucca* ride

Cast off from the Corniche by hiring a *felucca* sailboat at the end of the afternoon. These white-sailed low-draughted craft ply their way effortlessly through the water. Drift lazily along the Nile as the setting sun slowly sinks behind the Valley of the Kings.

7.00pm Evening entertainment

Take a horse-drawn *calèche* to Karnak Temple to experience the epic Sound and Light Show. Trotting along the Corniche just after sunset is a memorable experience. Ask the driver to wait for you to return to Luxor after the show.

9.00pm Dinner

An evening meal at one of the rooftop restaurants with sweeping views across the glimmering Nile is unforgettable. Afterwards, why not join the locals for a sheesha pipe and coffee.

17

35

57

CONTENTS

61

71

82

INTRODUCTION

The River Nile has long exercised a potent spell over ordinary people. Egypt, or someone's idea of it, has inspired poetry and literature, and styles in everything from Western architecture to paper packaging. A visit to Egypt is certainly memorable, but a cruise along the River Nile is an unforgettable experience. Travelling by boat gives a deeper understanding of the river and the culture of the people who have lived along its banks for centuries.

Visitors have cruised the Nile since Roman times, intrigued by the dusty remains of an ancient civilisation. Historically, it was only the wealthy who could afford the time and expense of a Nile cruise, but now the experience is easily within reach of anyone looking for the perfect combination of history, culture and adventure. Passing within a few metres of the riverbank, your view from the boat will give insights into the local culture that are impossible by any other means. After all, experiencing local village life is impossible from a speeding aeroplane. Enjoy the slower pace, as you wind your way up the river and back through history to an earlier time.

Egypt is a land of unusual geographic isolation, with well-defined boundaries. To the east and west are vast deserts, and to the north is the Mediterranean Sea. To the south there was – before the construction of the Aswan High Dam – a barrier of rock, beyond which lay the land of Nubia. Within these boundaries was a land divided; Upper Egypt extended from Aswan to a point just south of modern Cairo and was largely barren, apart from a narrow strip along the river; the Delta, or Lower Egypt, spread from the point where the Nile fanned into a fertile triangle some 200 km (125 miles) before

Cruising the Nile on board a *dahabiya* (river-going sailboat)

The Nile's Journey

The River Nile has two main tributaries. The White Nile flows from Lake Victoria in Central Africa through Uganda and Sudan before joining the Blue Nile at Khartoum. The Blue Nile brings the greatest volume of water and silt from the Ethiopian Highlands, creating the rich and fertile soil of Egypt.

reaching the Mediterranean Sea. Linking Upper and Lower Egypt was the vital artery, the River Nile.

Choosing the Right Cruise

The crucial decision when planning a trip along the Nile is choosing the right boat. Whether excursions are offered, the crew's hospitality standards, and the temperament of your fellow passengers are all issues you should think about when choosing which of the 400 cruise boats will take you upriver. While many of the sightseeing itineraries are standard and based on the length of your cruise, make sure you have the time you need to see the sights that are particularly appealing. Also take into consideration your travel habits: drinks can be expensive on-board, so consider an all-inclusive deal if you enjoy an evening cocktail.

Timing your trip to get the best weather is also important. Spring and autumn are popular, offering sunny days and pleasant evenings. Winter has warm days and cool nights and is the busiest time, especially over Christmas and New Year, when historic sites can be extremely crowded. Summer is the quietest, but can get brutally hot, with temperatures reaching the upper-40s °C (upper-110s °F).

Most cruise itineraries are standard, and a seven-day cruise beginning and ending in Luxor is common. Typically, two days are spent traveling to Aswan (with sightseeing stops), and a single day spent sailing back to Luxor. Most of the nights are actually spent moored in Luxor or Aswan, due to the number of important sites at both places. If time is of an essence, it is possible to split this into a four-day Luxor-Aswan cruise or three-day Aswan-Luxor cruise. Sightseeing excursions from the boats are normally included in your package, although a tight sailing schedule sometimes means you won't have the luxury of time to appreciate the amazing sites.

Due to size restrictions on the locks and bridges along the river, most Nile cruise boats are quite small, often with less than 100 guests. Tour companies sometimes sell the same cruise in many countries, so the final mix of passengers could be quite diverse. Use the boat list in this book to find information about a particular boat and its itinerary *(see page 123)*. Of course, the general rule is that the more expensive crusies offer a better experience in terms of the quality of the boat, service and food.

Musicians accompany belly dancers and Sufi spinners

Extensions

To truly experience all that Egypt has to offer, many visitors choose to extend their visit. Spending a few extra days in Cairo before you join the boat offers the chance to see the Pyramids, the Egyptian Museum, the Khan Al Khalili bazaar and Old Cairo. On the other end, a further cruise on Lake Nasser or a transfer to Hurghada or Sharm Al Sheikh to relax and enjoy the Red Sea gives you a well-rounded trip to Egypt. An extra week in a Luxor hotel will provide ample opportunities to see the other ancient sites on the West Bank whilst sampling more of Upper Egypt.

A Typical Day Aboard

A typical day on your Nile cruise boat usually starts quite early. Breakfast is served around 7am for a quick 7.30am departure to the day's selected site, which is best seen before

Early evening is one of the most peaceful times on the river

the temperature gets too high. Security is managed by issuing a boat pass as you depart, which will allow only current passengers back onboard that evening. It also confirms that everyone has returned before the boat sets sail. Returning from the site visit mid-morning allows plenty of time for relaxing on the sun deck or taking a dip in the pool.

Passengers are expected to change out of swimwear for lunch, served around 1pm in the restaurant. The sailing schedule might allow for another site visit after lunch, with afternoon tea/coffee adjusted accordingly. Cruising along the Nile in the late afternoon is a real delight, when the heat of the day has passed and the sun is casting long shadows. Looking west towards the setting sun, the river sometimes looks like liquid silver, its smoothness only interrupted by the reflected silhouette of local a palm tree or fisherman.

Pre-dinner drinks in the bar is the time to reflect on your Nile adventure and catch up with your fellow passengers. Formal dressing for dinner is only expected on the most upmarket of boats and will be indicated in the instructions when you join the cruise. Otherwise casual evening wear is acceptable, but some occasions are a great excuse to dress up for dinner. Evening meals are the opportunity for the chef and kitchen staff to show off with extravagant displays of food and elaborate presentations of ingredients. Spread over four or five courses, the relaxed evening meal can easily take two hours or more.

After the evening meal there might be a special show of Egyptian belly dancing, Sufi spinning, local musicians or a more informal night of song and dance organised by the staff. For those with any energy left, the decks at night are fabulous places to watch the world go by, drifting along on the inky blackness of the world's longest river. Then retire to your comfortable cabin, ready to start all over again tomorrow.

A BRIEF HISTORY

Egypt produced one of the earliest and most magnificent civilisations the world has ever witnessed. Five thousand years ago, when Mesopotamia was still the scene of petty squabbles between city states and while Europe, America and most of western Asia were inhabited by Stone-Age hunters, the ancient Egyptians had learned how to make bread, brew beer and mix paint. The could smelt and cast copper, drill beads, mix mineral compounds for cosmetics, and glaze stone and pottery surfaces. They had invented the hoe, the most ancient of agricultural implements, and had carried out experiments in plant and animal breeding.

The earliest human inhabitants of the Nile Valley were hunters who tracked game across northern Africa and eastern Sudan, later joined by Nomadic tribes of Asiatic origin. Their lives were bound to the ebb and flow of the annual flood. As the water rose each year in July, the inhabitants were obliged to draw back from the banks. By October the river began to subside, leaving lagoons and streams that became natural reservoirs for fish.

Riverside villages developed along the Nile during the Badarian period (5500–4000BC) followed by a larger pottery-producing settlement at Naqad, near modern-day Qena. Goods often travelled down the river from the south to Elephantine Island, where the route was disrupt-

Nile cataracts

'Cataract' comes from the Greek word for waterfall, and refers to a series of dangerous rocks and fast-flowing water in Upper Egypt. Traditionally there were six cataracts, numbered as they were encountered going up the Nile. The first is at Aswan, whilst the second at Wadi Halfa now lies below Lake Nasser, the artificial lake behind the Aswan Dam.

ed by cataracts (*see box*). The island became a link with trade routes to the ancient Red Sea ports of Berenice and Myos Hormos, as well as an important tax collecting and military base.

In around 3100BC King Menes of Upper Egypt defeated the states of Lower Egypt to unite Egypt. He became the first king of the 1st dynasty, ruling from a new city called Memphis. Menes is the first king to be portrayed wearing both the white crown of Upper Egypt and the red crown of Lower Egypt.

Middle and New Kingdoms

Mentuhotep, a king of the Middle Kingdom's 11th dynasty, control to the south and developed Thebes (now known as Luxor) into a strong religious and political centre in 2000BC. Amenemhet I, whose rule heralded a revival in ar-

Early picture of the Temple of Amun-Re at Karnak

chitecture and the arts, established the 12th dynasty, one of the most peaceful and prosperous eras in Egyptian history. At the end of the 12th dynasty the provincial rulers once again rose against the crown. It was during this time that the Hyskos challenged Egyptian authority. With the assistance of horses and chariots (which were hitherto unknown in Egypt), the Hyskos had a devastating effect and conquered the country.

The humiliation of foreign occupation came to an end when Ahmose, father of the New Kingdom (18–20th dynasties) started a war of liberation and finally expelled the hated invaders (1570–1070BC).The names of the 18th- and 19th-dynasty pharaohs are still familiar to visitors today – Amenhotep, Thutmose, Tutankhamunm and Ramses II. Apart from the heretical king Akhenaten, they concentrated their power in Thebes, turning it into the largest religious building ever constructed.

For the afterlife, each pharaoh built a greater tomb than his predecessor. The tombs in the Valley of the Kings were decorated and supplied for the pharaoh's journey after death. Enormous funerary temples were constructed, carved with the triumphs of the great military pharaohs who plundered Nubia and Kush (Sudan) in the south, Canaan, Syria and Phoenicia in the north.

In the 7th century BC, the 25th dynasty was ruled by kings from Nubia and Kush and Ethiopia. In 525BC, Egypt was plundered by King Darius, whose Persian successors ruled Egypt on and off for 200 years. It was

Thebes' West Bank

The city of Thebes and Karnak Temple were on the East Bank of the Nile – the land of the living – as represented by the rising sun. The West Bank where the sun set was the land of the dead – the site of the famous Theban necropolis and the Valley of the Kings.

during this time of Persian rule that one of the most famous historians, Herodotus, visited Egypt, in around 450BC. The Greek writer and traveller gives us the earliest account of Egypt's grandeur, describing the work of the temple priests. Because of these writings, we know that their rituals are still performed in much the same way as at the time of the great pharaohs.

From the Greeks to Islam

The Mediterranean port of Alexandria was founded for, named after, and planned by Alexander the Great when his army conquered Egypt. Upon his death, his Greek generals established their own pharaobic dynasty known as the Ptolomies. Their greatest legacies are the magnificent temples at Edfu, Kom Umbo and Philae. The last Greek ruler was the famous Queen Cleopatra. Her legendary love affairs with both Julius Caesar and Mark Antony have provided fodder for writers ever since. After her suicide-by-asp in 30BC, Egypt became a minor province within the Roman Empire.

Christianity appeared in Egypt in the first century AD, when the apostle Mark preached in Alexandria. Isolated desert monasteries were established and early

Pompey's Pillar and sphinx at the remains of Serapeum

Christians defaced the imagery on ancient Egyptian temples before converting them to churches. Queen Hatshepsut's funerary temple is still known by its Christian name of Dye Al Bahari (the Northern Monastery). As part of the Eastern Roman Empire, Egypt was eventually ruled by the Byzantines in Constantinople, but theological differences led to the creation of the Patriarch of Alexandria as head of the Coptic Orthodox Church.

In AD641 raiders from Arabia brought the Islamic faith into Egypt and altered the country forever. It was the Arabs who renamed Thebes as Al Uqsur (Luxor) or 'the palaces', referring to the ancient temples and great buildings.

The early years of Islam were dominated by the religion's expansion across North Africa. Under successive Islamic rulers, Egypt was controlled by a series of regional governors and languished as a regional province. Over the next thousand years, the Mamluks, who were originally brought to Egypt as Turkish soldier slaves, grew in strength and eventually came to power.

Serapeum remains, Alexandria

In 1517 Egypt was absorbed into the mighty Ottoman Empire. Cairo became a flourishing city thanks to the booming coffee industry, which shipped beans up the Red Sea from the port of Mocha in Yemen.

The Europeans Arrive

Napoleon's army arrived in Egypt in 1798. Despite French control lasting only a few years, Upper Egypt would never be the same.

Along with troops and weapons, the French brought intellectuals and artists, keen to witness firsthand the wonders of Ancient Egypt. In 1799 they unearthed the Rosetta Stone which was inscribed in three languages: Ancient Egyptian hieroglyphics, a later demotic text, and Greek. The new field of archaeology brought knowledge and understanding to the ancient monuments, especially after the French Egyptologist Champollion deciphered hieroglyphics in 1822 using the Rosetta Stone and papyrus scrolls.

Hieroglyphics on a temple wall at Karnak, Luxor

Muhammad Ali Pasha is credited for having laid the foundations of modern Egypt. In 1805 he realised that Egypt could only progress using European knowledge and technology. He built schools, constructed barrages across the Nile, encouraged cotton growing with new irrigation techniques and developed a high-grade cotton industry that is still acknowledged as producing one of the world's finest textiles.

By the 19th century, Upper Egypt became a destination for scholars and adventurers keen to capture the essence of Ancient Egypt, but sometimes they did more than that. Opportunists such as Giovanni Belzoni (collecting for the British Museum) and Bernardino Drovetti (collecting for the

French) stripped the temples of any object that could be moved. Some of the pieces taken by Belzoni, including the colossal head of 'Young Memnon' (actually Rameses II), are still on display at the British Museum.

The Victorian artist David Roberts popularised Egypt with his wonderful depictions of ruined temples. He undertook a journey lasting eleven months in 1838–9, sailing as far south as Abu Simbel. The British travel writer Amelia Edwards also drew attention to Egypt by bringing her Nile adventures into the living rooms of Victorian Britain by publishing her enormously successful *A Thousand Miles Up the Nile* in 1876.

Fearful of the effect that so many tourists would have upon the ancient sites, Edwards co-founded the Egypt Exploration Fund to study antiquities and promote Egyptology. One scholar who benefited from her patronage was

A Thomas Cook tour to the Pyramids in Victorian times

Flinders Petrie, a man who worked at Naqada and also recorded thousands of ancient inscriptions on Sahel Island in Aswan. Later scholars continued his work, including the well-known Howard Carter.

The Taming of the Nile

While Muhammad Ali's descendants oversaw the building of new railways and the Suez Canal, Britain took control over Egypt in 1882. Aswan became an important staging post for Lord Kitchener's relief of Khartoum in 1898, for which he was later rewarded with the gift of the island that now bears his name. Engineers worked to harness the mighty Nile river by building dams, barrages and canals to irrigate more land. By controlling the yearly floods of the Nile River, the people of Egypt were able to harness the power of the Nile for their own purposes.

Discovering King Tut's Tomb

By 1922 the general consensus was that the Valley of the Kings was exhausted and all the tombs of the pharaohs had been discovered. However, Howard Carter, who had been searching since 1914, remained confident there was more to find. But this 1922 season would be the last that his benefactor Lord Carnarvon could finance. A workman uncovered a cut step that had been hidden under stones of a ruined hut for over 3,000 years. Clearing the steps on 4 November, Carter found a sealed door, miraculously undamaged. He waited three weeks for Carnarvon to arrive before breaking through the door into a small sloping corridor filled with rubble. Once cleared, the passage led them to another intact doorway with the royal seal of Tutankhamun guarding the antechamber. Making a small hole in the door, Carter allowed his eyes to adjust to the darkness whilst Carnarvon eagerly waited. 'Can you see anything?' Carnarvon asked. 'Yes, wonderful things' replied Carter.

The archaeologist Howard Carter's Luxor home

By the turn of the century, archaeologists were coming to Egypt to uncover the past. Howard Carter's discovery of the great tomb of King Tutankhamun in 1922 ranks as one of the greatest discoveries ever made. It was headline news around the world. Fascination with Egypt has reigned ever since, and tourists continue to flock to Egypt's Valley of the Kings.

Independence

Preceded by nationalistic riots, the last descendent of Muhammad Ali, King Farouk, was deposed when the British were ousted in the military coup of 1952. Gamal Abdul Nasser became President and nationalised the Suez Canal. The Suez crisis in 1956 was a British, French and Israeli attempt to seize the canal, which ended in failure. Egypt fought the State of Israel in several short wars over the Sinai Peninsula until the signing of the Camp David Peace Accord by Nasser's successor, Anwar Sadat. Growing internal problems led to the assassination of Sadat during a military parade in 1981. His vice-president Hosni Mubarak assumed leadership. He has tried to promote a more democratic government, but his greatest challenge has come from Islamic fundalmentalists. He has negotiated Egypt through the troubled waters of Middle Eastern politics since 1981.

Historical Landmarks

250,000BC Stone tools discovered in Upper Egypt.
13,000BC Evidence of early Nile Valley civilisations.
5500BC Start of Badarian period of early pre-dynastic settlements in Upper Egypt.
4000BC Naqada becomes a centre for Upper Egypt.
3100BC Upper and Lower Egypt unified with new capital at Memphis.
2780BC–2270BC Old Kingdom period.
2133BC–1785BC Middle Kingdom period.
1575BC–1085BC New Kingdom period.
c.1352BC The boy king Tutankhamun dies and is buried in his tomb.
c.1279BC Rameses II begins a reign lasting around 67 years.
c.450BC Greek historian Herodotus travels in Egypt.
332–30BC Greek Ptolomies build new temples at Edfu, Kom Umbu and Philae.
30BC The Romans add Egypt to their trading empire.
1st century AD Christianity brought to Egypt by St Mark.
4th century AD Early Coptic monasteries established.
641 Arab invaders under Amr Ibn Al Aas bring Islam to Egypt.
1171 Salah Addin adds Egypt to his growing Ayyubid Empire.
1798 Napoleon's troops conquer Egypt.
1822 Jean Francois Champollion deciphers ancient hieroglyphic texts.
1922 Howard Carter and Lord Carnarvon discover the undisturbed tomb of Tutankhamun.
1952 King Farouk abdicates and British control is ended.
1956 Gamal Abdul Nasser becomes President, the Suez Canal crisis occurs and Sudan gains independence.
1960s Abu Simbel rescued from the rising waters of Lake Nasser.
1971 High Dam at Aswan completed and opened by President Sadat.
1981 President Sadat assassinated, Hosni Mubarak becomes President.
2005 Inhabitants of Qurna (village near Valley of Kings) told to leave their houses, which are built over ancient tombs.
2010 The Avenue of Sphinxes emerges from beneath Luxor.

WHERE TO GO

The region of Upper Egypt between Luxor and Aswan contains perhaps a greater concentration of renowned historical sites than anywhere else in the world. While your cruise boat is moored at Luxor, you can explore the riches of Valley of the Kings and the majestic Karnak and Luxor temples; during the Aswan stop-off you will be able to see the architectural feats of Abu Simbel and the High Dam up close.

During your cruise, discover the wonderful riverside temple at Kom Ombo, the stunningly well-preserved temple of Edfu and, of course, the magic of the River Nile itself. Guided excursions are normally included in the cost of your cruise, and usually operate within quite a strict timetable.

As well as these attractions, this chapter details many other important sites, some of which you might only be able to visit by adding a few extra days at the start or end of a Nile cruise.

LUXOR–EDFU CRUISE

The logistics of tour itineraries, charter flight arrivals, Esna lock access and overnight mooring means that many boats depart Luxor around lunchtime each day. Each group will have done some sightseeing in the morning, and lunch is taken as you set off on your Nile cruise. Sailing along this particular stretch of river can seem like a race to get to Esna Lock, but there are much quieter sections later. Over the next few years, all Nile cruise boats will be moved away from central Luxor to the area around the bridge. Many tour companies have bought Nile-side plots and developed them into smart secure arrival and departure areas within landscaped gardens.

Luxor at dusk

Leaving Luxor

All boats initially head towards a large mountain called **Jabal Al Rakhamiyya**, rising 600m (1,970ft) above the
1 Nile. Beyond the first large island is the town of **Armant**, about 17km (10½ miles) south of Luxor. Today the most dominant feature is the large sugar refinery used for processing the sugar cane of the region *(see box below)*. This was the site of ancient Hermonthis, with a temple dedicated to both Jupiter and his son Apollo, according to the Greek geographer Strabo who visited around 25BC probably just after the temple was built. Opposite Armant on the eastern side of the river are the remains of ancient Al Tawd, at the foot of the distant hills *(see page 71)*. Stone blocks pillaged from its Montu Temple were used in the building of the sugar refinery.

The river now bends south around the end of the mountain. Just beyond Al Dimugrat on the western bank is a new

Armant Sugar Factory

Strange as it may seem, not everyone in Upper Egypt is involved with tourism. The growing, transportation and refining of sugar cane has been the major industry in the region for over 150 years. In relatively poor areas like Armant, the factory is at the heart of the community and directly employs about 20,000 people during the main 'juicing' season. The cut lengths of cane are transported on open-sided wagons along hundreds of kilometres of narrow-gauge railways that snake along the West Bank. Built in 1855, the factory lies idle for most of the year as the crop grows but once the harvest has started in December, the smoke can be seen for many kilometres up and downstream until May. Egypt produces the sweetest sugar in the world, with maximum sweetness being achieved between January and April. By-products are used to make wood and paper as well as certain perfumes and alcohol.

boatyard where some of the cruise boats are refurbished and maintained, rather than in Cairo. Several boats will be hoisted clear of the water and it is easy to see how shallow the draft is, sometimes as little as 1.5m (5ft).

As the river narrows between the rocky outcrops, look out for the small tomb of a holy man known as Sheikh Musa at the top of **Jabalein** (meaning 'two mountains') on the West Bank, 300m/yds from the river. Below this and out of sight are the ruins of ancient Crocodilopolis (dedicated to the crocodile-headed God Sobek) and Aphroditopolis (where the cow-headed God Hathor was worshipped).

Another 7km (4 miles) further on, but this time on the eastern bank, are some tombs that can just be seen above the treetops about 600m/yds away. These are at **Al Ma'allah** and pre-date the Theban necropolis by more than 500 years. Leaving the mountain behind, the route is now due south to-

Esna is home to some handsome old buildings

Haggling at Esna

wards **Esna**, the suburbs of which start to appear on the western side before reaching the lock, about 4–5 hours after leaving Luxor. 2

Delays of around 30 minutes to two hours to get into the lock at Esna are common. As the boats wait, enterprising vendors row out to offer dresses, *galabiyas*, shirts and scarves. Most cabin windows do not open, so the only way to inspect the goods is to get them thrown onto the sundeck, which the sellers do with great gusto and accuracy. Any unwanted goods are returned overboard: if anything ends up in the river it is fished out and quickly dried. Haggling over the price is quite interesting at a vertical distance of 12m (39ft). If a sale is agreed, pop the money in the bag and throw it down with the rejects; or sometimes you'll be thrown a small canister to stuff the notes into. Unless you are very accurate, try not to put too many coins into the payment bag, otherwise it sinks without trace.

Esna Locks

With the exception of the new longer cruise boats of over 80m (260ft), two boats can fit into each of Esna's **two locks**, which are 160m (525ft) by 17m (55ft). The eastern lock was originally built when the new barrage was constructed between 1989 and 1994. The newer western lock is identical and was opened in 2007, meaning that there are no longer total closures for maintenance and allowing boats to cruise year-round. A small hydropower plant is located beside the lock with an 85MW capacity (the Aswan High Dam can generate up to 2100MW). The boats push the size restrictions to the limit, as they all barely squeeze into the lock and fit under the road bridge. Some even exceed the permitted height, with shade awnings and masts that swing down flat along the deck to get under the bridges. Once inside the lock, the boats rise up around 6m (20ft), an operation that is swiftly and efficiently handled.

Exiting the lock is not the end of the restrictions. A kilometre south of the new barrage is the old British-built **barrage** from 1908, designed to help distribute water for irrigation. Along its 900m/yd length, it had 120 openings, each of 5m/yds, with a lock at the western end to allow boats, barges and *feluccas* through. This older structure was replaced after it came under extra pressure when greater volumes of water were released from the High Dam at Aswan in the 1970s and '80s. The cruise boats still have to fit through the old lock but it no longer operates. Notice the discarded swing bridge by the side, which was the only road bridge across the Nile between Qena and Edfu until Luxor bridge was constructed in the 1990s. Beyond the abandoned lock is the new

Esna Lock

riverfront at Esna, backed by some fine buildings. Esna has been an important trading town for thousands of years – here several *wadi* valleys run towards the Nile from the Western Desert, along which Nubian and Sudanese traders have long brought camels.

Esna Temple

The town was known to the Ancient Egytians as Senet, and was the site of a temple constructed by Thutmose III and dedicated to the ram-headed God of creation, Khnum. The inhabitants were famous for worshipping the Latus fish, so the Greeks renamed the place Latopolis. The later **Roman Temple** (summer 7am–5pm, winter 7am–4pm; charge) of Emperors Claudius and Vespasian is now sunken into the ground at the heart of the modern souq, 200m/yds from the Nile. The only visible section is the great solid vestibule, whose walls are completely covered with carvings and texts. Some date from the 3rd century AD and are the last Ancient Egyptian texts to be written in hieroglyphics. Familiar Roman emperors such as Trajan, Domitian and Commodus are carved in typical Pharaonic poses, slaying enemies and making offerings.

The intricately carved exterior of Esna Temple

A visit to the temple, which is 1.5km (1 mile) beyond the old barrage, is not on every cruise itinerary but actually takes very little time.

Admiring Esna Temple

The river is a bit wider here; the eastern bank is characterised by huge banana plantations, whilst on the west, the suburbs of Esna give way to lush date palms and fields stretching all the way to Edfu. This part of the river always seems particularly quiet, with boats sailing singly or in pairs as they come through the lock. Large letters spell out 'Welcome to Aswan', referring to the governorate rather than the town, which is still more than 150km (93 miles) away. Along the tops of the distant eastern mountains are modern mining operations, below which – and closer to the river – are often the remains of older stone quarries.

Al Kab and Eileithyias

Some 33km (20miles) from Esna towards Edfu (roughly two hours' sailing time), and just outside the modern town of Al Mahamid, are **Al Kab** and the important remains of 3 ancient **Eileithyias**. The thick mud walls of the old town run along the eastern bank of the river, enclosing a compound that is over 500 sq m/yds. Foundations of New Kingdom temples are all that is left of this capital of the third nome (administrative district) of Upper Egypt and centre of a cult of worship of the vulture goddess Nekhbet. Beyond this are a series of tombs cut into the hillside dating from the Middle and New Kingdoms. Easily observed with binoculars from the boat is the modern stone staircase used to reach the **tombs of Ahmose**, a navy admiral who fought the Hyksos, and his nephew Pahery. Behind this are a series of *wadis* draining from the Eastern Desert that provide an overland shortcut north to Luxor and access to old gold mines.

Kom Al Ahmar to Edfu

On the western bank at this point, out of view beyond the
4 fields, are the important ruins of **Kom Al Ahmar** (Red Mountain). They are also known as **Hierakonopolis**, a Greek name meaning Falcon City, indicating the worship of the falcon-headed god Horus. This is ancient Nekhen, the capital of Upper Egypt possibly as far back as 4000BC. The site is where the famous Narmer palette *(see right)* was un-

Dresses for sale in Edfu

covered in 1898, named after the eponymous king. The same king might also have been King Menes, who first unified Upper and Lower Egypt *c.*3100BC. Kom Al Ahmar is also the site of the oldest-known painted and decorated Egyptian tomb.

Heading southwards once more is the large sugar refinery factory on the western bank at Al Kilh Gharb. Before reaching the dirty ferrosilicon production factory on the eastern bank, look to the southwest to see the huge entrance pylons of Edfu Temple looming over the town. After passing under the bridge, the boat will moor along the town's extensive riverside corniche. Edfu is about halfway between Luxor and Aswan.

The Narmer palette

This 5,000-year-old carved tablet is now in the Egyptian Museum in Cairo and is arguably the oldest historical document in existence. The heiroglyphics date from around 3,100BC and the tablet shows King Narmer wearing the crown of Upper Egypt on one side and of Lower Egypt on the other.

EDFU–ASWAN CRUISE

There is generally less river traffic on the second half of the cruise. Between the local mud houses are fields running down to the Nile, often home to water buffalo, camels and donkeys. This is a great opportunity to view the bird life along the riverbanks; most of the birds are easy to spot, such as egrets, herons, falcons and the wonderful pied kingfisher. If you are lucky you might see the vivid plumage of the Nile valley sunbird.

Edfu was the capital of the second nome of Upper Egypt, 5
whose history dates from the Old Kingdom. It developed at a point where a major trade route entered the Nile Valley from the Red Sea (today's Marsa Alam).

Edfu Temple

If anything remains of Edfu from this early period it is still buried under the modern town; though still remaining is the wonderful later Ptolemaic temple. By far the best preserved of all the temples, it is situated behind the town, requiring a bus or *calèche* transfer or a 20-minute walk along the main street from the cruise mooring. The recent demolition of nearby buildings gives space for this splendid temple to be appreciated as you pass around the exterior towards the entrance.

Begun around 237BC under Ptolemy III, **Edfu Temple** (summer 6am–5pm, winter 7am–4pm; charge) was dedicated to Horus and took about 180 years to construct. Its remarkable state of preservation is mainly due to being covered with sand and the roof used as a solid base for local housing, as shown in David Roberts' prints from 1838. The pylon (monumental gateway) is particularly striking in size and decoration. At 36m (118ft) high and almost 80m

Story of Horus

A great battle took place at Edfu between the gods Horus and Seth. According to the Ancient Egyptians, Horus was the son of Osiris and Isis (who were also brother and sister). He exacted revenge on his Osiris's murderer Seth to regain his rightful claim to be royal leader of the earth.

Horus was considered to be the principal royal god to whom the pharaohs had to make symbolic offerings. His carvings are on many temple walls and pylons (entrances) but his main centre of worship was here at Edfu. Part of the pharaohs' power came from the fact that they considered themselves to be 'living kings' as incarnations of Horus.

The four 'sons of Horus' were gods who protected the vital organs of the deceased, which were placed in four canopic jars – named after Canopus, a town in ancient Egypt about 20km (12 miles) east of Alexandria.

(260ft) wide, it is the second-largest after the one at Karnak *(see page 63)* and depicts pharaohs slaying enemies and offering gifts to the gods. Two fine black granite statues of Horus stand at the entrance. Passing through the entrance, look up at the winged solar disk that still retains some of its original blue, red and white colouring.

The courtyard is surrounded by a covered colonnade with beautifully carved columns and capitals. Twelve huge columns support the vestibule roof and the walls are inscribed with scenes of the foundation and consecration of the temple. Small chapels on either side served as a library and purification rooms. Later, Christians repainted some walls with images of saints and defaced some of the ancient carvings. Tourists cram the entrance to the inner sanctuary to view the black granite plinth and replica wooden barque. Allow enough time to walk around the exterior of the building and its open-air museum with carved blocks and statues, some relating to the Christian era. If visiting in the morning, the pylon facade will probably be in the shade, whereas the rear wall with its tremendous carvings of gods and kings will be bathed in sunlight.

Leaving Edfu, the river splits into narrower channels

The imposing exterior of Edfu Temple

A *calèche* makes its way through Edfu Town

to run around a string of large islands. Villages and houses are never far away, offering good close-up views of everyday life from your boat – even better with binoculars.

Jabal As Silsilah

About 40km (25 miles) south of Edfu, the mountains squeeze the river through a narrow channel at **Jabal As** 6
Silsilah. The meanings of this site's various names have been lost over time, but the most likely translation is 'stone wall', referring to the worked quarries on either side. Compared to the limestone further north, the sandstone here is easier to cut and relatively simple to transport, being so near to the Nile.

The quarries on the eastern side were extensively worked even up until the last century, supplying the stones for the old Esna barrage. The quarries on the western bank show a great deal of carved decoration with the intimate **Temple of Horemheb** at the top of a small flight of steps being the most impressive. The facade has four large entrances with a central doorway, several statue niches and carvings of the king along the prepared rock face. The role of the Nile in the stone-cutting process was never forgotten, as several small temples appear to have been built in worship of the river. *Feluccas* and *dahabiyas* can be moored alongside for visiting the riverside temples and extensively worked quarries. Cruise boats cannot stop here, but it is a wonderful experience to slowly sail past the carved and decorated shrines cut directly from the rock. Towards the end of this parade is a peculiar monolith known as the **'Capstan'**, a single square-cut pillar left exposed below a natural rock cap.

Once through Jabal As Silsilah, the landscape opens up on the eastern side with a large irrigated area almost 30km (19 miles) long. This fertile region greatly expanded in the 1960s when thousands of Nubians moved in, displaced by the construction of the High Dam on their homelands. The new villages were built as far as possible in the same style as their previous settlements. Agricultural production is high, with yet more sugar cane destined for the refinery at the next town of Kom Umbo. Boats swing east into this fertile area and then run straight towards the famous temple, which can be seen 3km (2 miles) away.

Kom Umbo

The temple at **Kom Umbo** (summer 6am–5pm, winter 7am 7
4pm; charge) was especially important throughout history, as it sought to appease one of the great dangers of living along the Nile – crocodiles. Perched high above the river, one half of the temple is dedicated to the crocodile-headed god Sobek. Some historians believe that live crocodiles might well have been kept here and allowed to wander around the temple. Extremely large mummified crocodiles have been discov-

Kom Umbo temple

Functional design

Only the chief priest was allowed into the inner sanctuary of the temple. However, what he said to the gods was relayed outside, as the temple acted as a giant megaphone with the ceiling getting higher towards the entrance: Kom Umbo, Edfu and Karnak are prime examples of this.

ered in side chapels, some of which are now displayed at the Mummification Museum at Luxor *(see page 69)* and the Egyptian Museum in Cairo. The other half of the temple is dedicated to the falcon-headed god Haroeris (an ancient form of Horus). The two halves are in identical buildings either side of a central line through the temple.

Much of the roof is missing so it is less claustrophobic than other enclosed temples. The quality and subject matter of the inscriptions are of great interest, featuring the most complete example of an Ancient Egyptian calendar and a display of medical instruments used for mummification. Note the scene depicting the purification of the king, where the stream of water is actually a string of small *ankhs* (keys of life).

About one hour's cruising south of Kom Umbo, the road and railway hug the eastern riverbank at the foot of splendid sandstone cliffs for about 3km (2 miles). Some 27km (17 miles) from Kom Umbo, a large fertile valley runs east from the river. This valley was one of the major natural highways that linked the Red Sea with the Nile in antiquity, with examples of ancient rock carvings along its course.

The approach into Aswan is signalled by the futuristic cable-stayed bridge, opened in 2002 and located 13km (8 miles) north of the city. Its construction was vital in the development of the Toshka and New Valley projects running from Lake Nasser. It is an impressive sight to pass beneath, especially when illuminated at night. Once through, the river curves around a sandy outcrop topped by a small tomb (Qubbet Al Hawa) to reveal Aswan.

ASWAN

Sun-scorched **Aswan** developed as a great trading centre on 8
the treacherous first cataract of the Nile, and today has a pleasant atmosphere where things are not done in a hurry. There is plenty to keep tourists occupied. One day is normally taken up visiting Abu Simbel; a popular half-day tour included in most cruises is a visit to Philae Temple, the two dams and the unfinished obelisk.

Philae Temple

The construction of the lower Old Aswan Dam *(see page 42)* in 1898–1902 allowed the floodwaters to pass through every summer, bringing water and silt to the fields of Egypt. For the rest of the year most sluices were shut to create a lake that flooded the upstream Nile Valley. Nearby **Philae Tem-** A

Aromatherapy oils for sale in Aswan

ple (summer 7am–5pm, winter 7am–4pm; charge), built on an island in the Nile, was thus half-submerged for much of the year, and visitors could sail *feluccas* in and around the temple buildings.

The construction of the High Dam meant that the lake between the two dams would always be full and the temple permanently half-submerged. Therefore, a remarkable joint effort by Unesco and Egypt's Supreme Council of Antiquities relocated the temple to higher grounds, and even landscaped its new home, the nearby island of Agiliqiyyah, to resemble Philae. All the monuments were meticulously rebuilt stone by stone, according to their original design and layout, finally opening to the public in 1980.

The visit to Philae begins at the wonderfully chaotic motor launch harbour at the eastern end of the Old Dam. Hundreds of boats jostle for access as boatmen yell at each

Philae Temple

other, all trying to squeeze into the few moorings along the slipway to collect their tour groups. Out on the lake are great views of the Old Dam, islands and birdlife.

Philae in Dorset

Two obelisks once stood in front of Philae Temple. The intact eastern obelisk was removed by explorer and Egyptologist William Bankes in 1821, and placed in his garden at Kingston Lacy, Dorset. The cartouche of Cleopatra III carved on the obelisk was one of the links that helped to decode hieroglyphic texts.

Built during the reign of the Ptolemies, the main structure of the temple is dedicated to the goddess Isis and approached along an open courtyard flanked by columns with floral capitals; on the right-hand side are columns that were never finished. Ahead is the finely decorated first pylon, followed by a small courtyard with the **Mammisi** (Birth House) to the left. The second pylon is not aligned with the first, probably because the first was added later and had to shift position to fit onto the original island. The **Hypostyle Hall** of eight large columns was converted into a church by Emperor Justinian *c.*557AD, and several Christian motifs and carvings can be seen. The main sanctuary and its surrounding rooms are a little dark and claustrophobic, but depict impressive reliefs. Around the edge of the island are other buildings (a nilometer, the Temple of Augustus, the Roman Town Gate and the Temple of Hathor), but probably the most famous is the elegant **Kiosk of Trajan**, used as an official gateway to the temple when religious processions arrived at the island.

The boat ride, location and relative quiet make this a wonderful excursion. Revisiting the temple for the evening sound and light show *(see page 90)* is a completely different experience.

Aswan High Dam

Old Aswan Dam

The road to the High Dam and the airport passes across the top of the **Old Aswan Dam**. This British-built dam was the largest in the world when it opened in 1902 with 180 sluice gates and a length of 2km (1 mile). A lock at the western end allowed boats to continue south past the dam. Taming the Nile proved difficult and the dam was almost breached several times before its height was raised, first in 1912 and then again in 1933.

Crossing the Old Aswan Dam today offers great views downstream over the first cataract, where the hard granite outcrops split the Nile into fast-flowing rapids. Three kilometres (2 miles) north of the old dam are two small uninhabited islands designated as a nature reserve in 1986: **Saluga** (meaning 'cataract' in Nubian language) and **Ghazal** ('gazelle') offer refuge to Egyptian foxes, 60 species of birds and some unique desert plants.

Aswan High Dam

Even though the height of the Old Aswan Dam had been raised, another close call in 1946 showed that a completely new, even higher dam was needed. Independence and Cold War politics dictated that the Soviet Union, and not the British, would build this new High Dam during the 1960s.  Known locally as 'Sadd Al Aali', the **High Dam** (summer 7am–5pm, winter 7am–4pm; charge) is essentially a giant mountain placed in the way of the river, and the statistics are mind-blowing. Almost 1km (½ mile) thick at the base, over 100m (328ft) in height and 3.6km (2¼ miles) long, it needed 42.7 million cubic metres (½ billion cubic feet) of material to complete. Lake Nasser, which formed behind it, is over 500km (311 miles) in length. Tourists no longer visit the spiky monument to Soviet-Egyptian friendship, nor the hydro-electric plant, but stop along the middle of the dam. Lake Nasser cruise boats can be seen in the port to the east, whilst New Kalabshah and its collection of rescued temples are on an island to the southwest *(see page 52)*. Sometimes photography is not allowed here.

Northern Quarry

The granite strata responsible for the first cataract is also quarried and carved into blocks, statues and obelisks. Several places around Aswan have produced red, rose or pink granite and the most famous, D **Northern Quarry** (8am–4pm; charge), still contains a huge block that was once destined to be Egypt's largest obelisk. Three sides of the obelisk had been cut away and roughly prepared when it was abandoned in 1500BC, possibly because of a fracture. If fully quarried it would have been over 40m (130ft) in height and weighed more than 1,100

A massive unfinished obelisk resides at the Northern Quarry

Local stone

The type of granite hewn out of the quarries at Aswan is known as syenite. It is an igneous rock composed of alkali-rich feldspar and hornblende, generally with a pleasant rose or pink appearance from the mineral orthose. The name syenite comes from Syene, the Greek name for Aswan.

tons. The marked tourist trail shows how the blocks were split from the rock and remains of a narrow canal linked to the Nile for easy transportation downstream.

West Bank

You can undertake a half-day excursion by *felucca* or motor launch to visit the sites on the West Bank. From the summit of the Nobles' Tombs, it is a 30-minute camel trek or 45-minute walk across the sand to reach St Simeon's Monastery. The Aga Khan Mausoleum is passed when returning to the river. Further south along the bank are Nubian villages, popular with many visitors. *Felucca* boatmen can arrange any visits not included as part of your cruise.

Tombs of the Nobles

E ▸ The **Tombs of the Nobles** (8am–4pm; charge; no camera) are dotted over the sandy hillside below the impressive landmark that is the later **Qubbet Al Hawa** ('Tomb of the Father of Wind'). The excavated tombs belong to dignitaries of the Old and Middle Kingdoms, who ruled from Elephantine Island *(see page 47)*.

The ramps you can see were used to drag the sarcophagi up from the river. The tombs here are older than the nobles' tombs near the Valley of the Kings, but the style is similar, featuring carvings and paintings of the deceased with family members and provisions for the afterlife. Some of the paintings are remarkable considering that they are almost 4,000 years old – especially those inside the tomb of Sirenput II (no.31).

St Simeon's Monastery

Simeon was a local saint of whom little is known. **St Simeon's Monastery** (8am–4pm; charge) is thought to have been started around the 6th century AD, extended 400 years later and abandoned in the 13th century. The ruins indicate a substantial complex of monastic buildings, including the main three-storied monastery, basilica, monks' cells and stables. Of interest are the kitchen, bakery, oil- and wine-presses and mill. The rock-cut caves were probably early living quarters. Its remoteness on the edge of the desert echoes the locations of other major Coptic monasteries in the north that are more difficult to reach. F

Aga Khan Mausoleum

The Aga Khan is the leader of the Ismaili sect of Shia Muslims. Born in 1877, Muhammad Shah spent the latter years of his life in Aswan for health reasons and was buried in the beautiful, simple G **Aga Khan Mausoleum** in 1959. His wife, the Begum Aga Khan, lived in the white villa below until her death in 2000 when her body was placed alongside his in a marble sarcophagus. Sadly, this Fatimid-inspired building is no longer open to the public.

The Qubbet Al Hawa presides over the Tombs of the Nobles

Nubian Village

Getting an invite into an Egyptian house is a real eye-

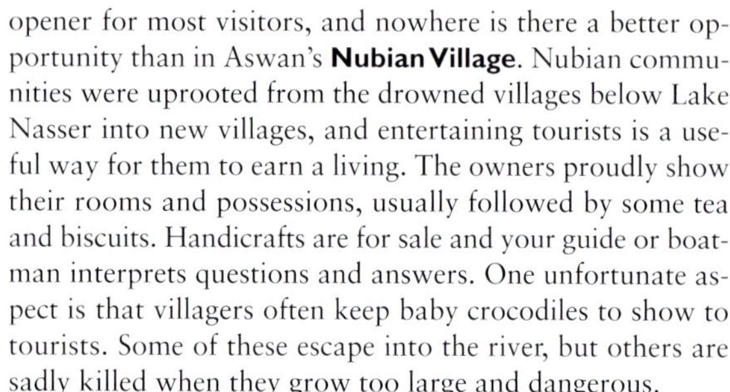

opener for most visitors, and nowhere is there a better opportunity than in Aswan's **Nubian Village**. Nubian communities were uprooted from the drowned villages below Lake Nasser into new villages, and entertaining tourists is a useful way for them to earn a living. The owners proudly show their rooms and possessions, usually followed by some tea and biscuits. Handicrafts are for sale and your guide or boatman interprets questions and answers. One unfortunate aspect is that villagers often keep baby crocodiles to show to tourists. Some of these escape into the river, but others are sadly killed when they grow too large and dangerous.

The Islands

A pleasant couple of hours can be spent sailing gracefully around the islands in a *felucca*. The most popular destinations are Elephantine and Kitchener Islands and the Nubian villages on the West Bank; or embark on a longer sail south

Aswan and the Size of the Earth

In 220BC, the Greek mathematician Eratosthenes used a hole in the ground in Aswan to calculate the circumference of the earth.

Aswan is almost on the Tropic of Cancer, so the sun shone directly down a vertical well at noon on Midsummer's Day. Eratosthenes measured the angle of the shadow cast by a stick (about seven degrees) in Alexandria at exactly the same time. This gave him Alexandria's angle of latitude, as it is almost due north of Aswan. All he needed then was the overland distance to Aswan to calculate the circumference of the earth. He asked camel traders how many days it took them to ride to Aswan and measured how far they travelled each day. He calculated it to be about 800km (500 miles), giving him a circumference of the earth of 46,000km (28,600 miles). The distance is actually c.40,000km (25,000 miles), but it was a pretty good calculation using just wells, sticks and camels over 2,000 years ago.

for a few hours through the lower cataracts to Sahel Island, passing the nature reserve islands of Saluga and Ghazal.

Elephantine Island

The main island opposite the corniche is **Elephantine Island**, 1
which is split into three distinct sections. At the northern end is the upmarket **Mövenpick Resort Aswan** with its own transfer boats and landing stage; in the centre is the local village accessed by public ferry; and at the southern end are ancient remains and the **Aswan Museum** (8am–4pm; charge), the former colonial home of Sir William Willcocks, the British designer of the Old Aswan Dam. Today it houses a dusty collection telling the history of the island; some of the finer items have been sent to the impressive new Nubia Museum *(see page 49)*. The annexe behind the main building has better displays of papyrus, pottery figures and bowls, hunting

Elephantine Island's Mövenpick Resort Aswan

A stroll on Kitchener Island

throw-sticks (boomerangs) and finds from the nearby Temple of Satet (goddess of fertility), built by Sesostris I during the 12th dynasty.

The archaeological site is a jumble of ruined buildings from various periods, even though the island was once the important capital of the first nome of Egypt, whose local rulers are buried in the Tombs of the Nobles. The central terrace was the base of the Temple of Khnum, the ram-headed god, of which little remains but a gateway. Views upstream across the jagged islands of the cataract, and towards the Old Cataract Hotel, are magnificent. Alongside the river is the nilometer – a structure for measuring the water level of the Nile that here comprises steps running down to the water inside a sloping passageway.

Kitchener Island

Hidden from view behind Elephantine Island is the smaller

J ▸ **Kitchener Island** (summer 8am–6pm, winter 8am–5pm; charge). Awarded to the eponymous British General after his successful relief of Khartoum and defeat of the Mahdi's forces at the Battle of Omdurman in 1898, it is now a little haven of beauty and tranquillity. Anyone with an interest in exotic flora will enjoy strolling around the labelled trees and shrubs, and citrus, medicinal and odoriferous plants. Get dropped off at one end, walk through to the pleasant café and set sail from the other end.

Nubia Museum

K One of the best modern museums in Egypt, the **Nubia Museum** (9am–9pm; charge; camera but no flash; www.numibia.net/nubia) opened in 1997. Focusing on the region to the south of Aswan, much of which is now lost under the lake, it offers a winning combination of historical artefacts and in-depth explanations. Themed sections cover early human activity, Old, Middle and New Kingdom periods, Nubian dynasties and identity, the Greco-Roman era, Christianity, Islam, irrigation techniques, the High Dam and rescued temples. Some of the best small pieces from the submerged sites are gathered here, together with reconstructed chapels and tombs. Towards the end of the collection are exhibits on Nubian folklore, traditions, culture and lifestyle, and fishing dioramas with a selection of mummy cases. Allow at least a couple of hours. There is a good café upstairs.

Coptic Cathedral

L The large **Coptic Cathedral of St Michael** (6am–9pm; charge) with its two soaring towers is on the way to the Nubia Museum. The presence of St Simeon's monastery across the river testifies to the deep roots of Christianity in Aswan, based on the tradition that

The lovely interior of the Coptic Cathedral

the Holy Family travelled to Upper Egypt during their exile. This centrepiece for the Coptic community was only consecrated in 2006. It is located just around the corner from the **Fryal Park** (8am–10pm; nominal charge), offering great views of the river in peaceful landscaped gardens. Across the road behind the cathedral is a newly discovered ancient temple (though not currently open to visitors).

LAKE NASSER CRUISE

9 For many years after the construction of the High Dam, **Lake Nasser** was out of bounds. Other than a few local fishermen and the weekly public ferry slowly making its way to Wadi Halfa in Sudan, only a handful of fisheries experts were allowed onto the lake. In 1993 restrictions were lifted for a new boat to start weekly cruises from Aswan to Abu Simbel.

A Lake Nasser cruise boat

The distance is almost the same as sailing to Luxor, but that's where any similarity with a Nile cruise ends. This is a beautiful journey in a surreal and bleak landscape. Over 500km (310 miles) in length, Nasser is one of the world's largest man-made lakes, both by volume and surface area. Most itineraries take four days to sail to Abu Simbel, and the return trip three days, but generally the same sites are seen enroute (entry fees included).

Camels at Lake Nasser

Lake Nasser

A cruise on Lake Nasser is in stark contrast to cruising along the Nile. Gone are the lush green fields either side of the narrow river. No villages, roads, towns or people to spot as you sail past the peaks of inhospitable sandy-coloured mountains. Amongst this barren landscape, however, are signs of human habitation, not from today but from the past. Old temples that once overlooked the river were taken apart and rebuilt on higher ground, rescued from a premature drowning. Many temples, fortresses and tombs still remain submerged below the waters of Lake Nasser, along with countless villages and towns that were the heartland of Nubia.

Lake Nasser is perhaps most famous for the rebuilding of temples above the new shoreline. In particular, the Abu Simbel project captured the world's attention throughout the 1960s when the giant temple was cut up and re-assembled

A temple statue near Lake Nasser

in a dramatic race against time. Other temples were saved in the **'Nubian Monuments Project'** and assembled together in four main groups, making it easier for tourists to visit them during a Lake Nasser cruise. Historically, the series of Nubian fortresses were the most important structures, helping to protect the region from southern invaders. Built from mudbrick, it was impossible to save them and most have dissolved back to where they came, a layer of silt below the water. Most of the original fortresses, temples and villages were situated where *wadis* ran into the Nile, often controlling important trade routes, especially from the famous Nubian gold mines. The aspect and situation of each rescued stone temple have been maintained and protected as far as possible; the cruise boats moor offshore and use small tenders to reach the lakeside temples.

New Kalabshah

There are currently eight large Lake Nasser cruise boats that start their journeys from the small harbour at the eastern end of the High Dam. As soon as the boat leaves Sadd Al Aali terminal, it runs past the great bulk of the High Dam towards the first group of saved temples at a place called **New Kalabshah** (7am–5pm; charge). The main building is **Kalabshah Temple**, originally located about 45km (28 miles) south and the first monument to be moved in 1961. Entry to the courtyard is through the impressive pylon which forms part of the surrounding wall. This Greco-Roman temple was built upon older ruins and dedicated to Mandulis, a Nubian form of the god Horus with carvings of Ptolemaic and Roman rulers depicted as pharaohs. The original gateway to the temple was gifted to the people of West Germany, and is now in the Egyptian Museum, Berlin. 10

To the south of the temple and relocated to a promontory overlooking the lake is the quaint **Kiosk of Qertassi**. Similar to Trajan's Kiosk at Philae, this small building has delightful Hathor capitals and was originally located 30km (19 miles) south of here, beside sandstone quarries. Nearby is the removed outer section of the temple of **Garf Husein** (the rock-cut inner section was left in situ), originally about 80km (50 miles) south. Beyond the columns of the Mammisi (birth house) is a path up to another small shrine. This is **Bayt Al Wali**, meaning 'House of the Holy Man', comprising a narrow courtyard with some lovely reliefs. Built for Rameses II, it depicts him defeating Libyans and Syrians on the west wall and Ethiopians on the east wall. It originally came from the area of Abu Hor, 50km (31 miles) south.

Kalabshah Temple

To Wadi Al Allaqi

South from New Kalabshah is the vastness of Lake Nass-

Kiosk of Qertassi

er, with the old course of the Nile running along the lake bed. The mountains on the eastern side rise up to heights of 250m (820ft) and glow with wonderful colours and hues towards sunset; the western hills are much lower.

Two hours' sailing from New Kalabshah, the boat passes through **Bab Al Kalabshah** (Gateway of Kalabshah), the original site of the Temple of Debod, which was given to Spain and is now in the central park of Madrid. The smaller temple of nearby Tafa was given to the Dutch and is now inside the National Museum of Antiquities in Leiden.

The next narrow section is about 10km (6 miles) further south and a cause for celebration. Abu Hor headland lies on the **Tropic of Cancer**, where most cruise boats serve a courtesy drink as they enter the tropics. Then 14km (9 miles) further on, the boat passes over the site of the Temple of Dendur, now housed in the Metropolitan Museum of Art in New York as a gift to the USA. Some 80km (50 miles) south of the High Dam is the small village of Garf Husein on the western shore of the lake, whose rock-cut temple still rests on the bottom of the lake. The outer section was removed to New Kalabshah and an 8m (26ft) -high sandstone statue is now centrepiece of Aswan's wonderful Nubia Museum.

Another 20km (12 miles) further south are two thin headlands jutting out from the east, 15km (9 miles) apart. Between

them is the large inlet of Wadi Al Allaqi, which leads to a series of ancient gold mines. This remote area, totalling 30,000 sq km (11,600 sq miles), was declared the **Wadi Al Allaqi** 11
Nature Reserve in 1989 to protect desert flora and fauna. Dakkah Temple *(see page 56)* was originally located where this *wadi* met the Nile. The southerly headland is Jabal Al Muharaqqah, overlooking the original site of Muharaqqah temple *(see page 56)*.

From here, the lake enters a narrow section which must have been a spectacular gorge before the waters rose and even now is only 1.1km (⅔ mile) wide. The lake continues within the confines of the mountainous shores for over 40km (25 miles), but there is a stop to visit three temples regrouped together. Cruise boats moor at one of the small offshore islands, probably in the evening with the temples illuminated. It is hard to think of a more remote, yet starkly beautiful place than this.

A barren but beautiful landscape near Wadi As Sebu

Wadi As Sebu

Early next morning, you will make a visit to the first of
 the three temples; **Wadi As Sebu** (meaning 'valley of lions'), a rock temple set into a small hill and approached along an avenue of lion-headed sphinxes. Dedicated to Amun and Re-Horakhty,

it was one of the six Nubian temples built by Rameses II, but is now partially destroyed. Beside the entrance pylon is a statue of the king, leading to the main building with good carvings and evidence of later use as a Christian church. Broken statues and blocks lie abandoned in the sand. The walk over to Dakkah temple is almost 1km (½ mile) along a graded dirt track, but camels can be hired nearby.

Dakkah and Muharaqqah

The large pylons of the second temple at **Dakkah** can be seen for some distance as they were placed on a flattened hilltop. It was initially started by an Ethiopian ruler called Ergamenes, but most of what we see today is a Greco-Roman temple dating from the 3rd century BC and dedicated to the god Thoth, represented both as an ibis and a baboon. The monumental entrance was added by Emperor Augustus who is depicted as a pharaoh. Between Dakkah and the lake is the smaller rebuilt **Muharaqqah temple**, also dating from the Roman period. Many of its capitals remained unfinished, as at Philae Temple. One curious element is a spiral staircase leading to the roof of the colonnade, the only example anywhere in Egypt. 13

The temple at Dakkah is sited on a flattened hilltop

Amadah, Derr and Pennout

A further two rescued temples lie 25km (15½ miles) due west, but the boat has to complete a southern loop to reach them. Midway along the southern bank is the old site of **Korosko** where many ancient rock drawings and carvings were found, now removed to Aswan's Nubia Museum and Cairo.

Sunset near Amadah

The next shore excursion is to the temples of Amadah and Derr, and the painted tomb of Pennout. Offshore below the middle of the lake is the original site of
14 **Amadah**, moved as a complete building weighing 800 tons to its current location. Started by Thutmose III, the exterior is unappealing, but the interior walls are covered with wonderful painted reliefs.

Nearby, along a graded track is **Derr**, another rock temple built by Rameses II and dedicated to Amun-Ra. Only the lower legs of royal statues remain at the entrance, but inside are some excellent wall and column carvings depicting the success of the pharaoh's Nubian campaigns.

Those not wanting to walk the 500m/yds to the **tomb of Pennout** can travel by donkey cart or camel. The tomb is dug into the ground below a small pyramid-shaped hill and contains a simple chamber and niche. Pennout was a high official under Rameses VI, and is depicted in carvings and paintings with his wife and six sons. Further southwest is the original site of Derr and about 15km (9 miles)

Amadah Temple

onwards would have been the rock cut temple of Al Lessiya, now housed at Turin's Egyptian Museum in Italy.

Qasr Ibrim

Before reaching Abu Simbel the boats pass the Nubian fortress of **Qasr Ibrim**, unique as it still stands in its original position. For thousands of years this hilltop garrison town controlled all river trade from Africa's interior, used continuously by Egyptians, Nubians, Romans, Byzantines, Christians and Muslims up until 200 years ago. The original town would have been down by the river with tombs along its banks. One of the five chapels was rescued and is in Aswan's Nubia Museum. Today the lake waters rise high enough to isolate the fort as an island. The stone walls are in a poor state and visitors must now view it from the boat as landings are no longer permitted.

On the western side, 25km (15½ miles) beyond Qasr Ibrim, is a large inlet guarded on its northern side by the towering Jabal Al Sadd. This is the flooded **Wadi Toshka**, starting point of a vast project to release water from Lake Nasser into an overflow area known as the Toshka Lakes and thence northwards to provide water to irrigate the New Valley. After the vastness of the lake, Abu Simbel looks amazingly small as the boat swings around to bring the temples into view.

Abu Simbel

A massive international effort raised the world-famous **Sun Temple** (7am–5pm; charge) above the rising waters of the lake in the 1960s. Thousands of blocks weighing 20,000 tons were cut and then assembled 180m (590ft) above and 64m (210ft) back from the lake. In the 1970s tourists flew from Aswan on day trips to be met by local Nubian tour guides, many of whom had been part of that rescue team. They always began tours by thanking visitors for their money and help to save their monuments. Such sentimentality has disappeared over 50 years, but it is a remarkable engineering achievement that keeps Nubia on the (slightly redrawn) map.

15 We call it **Abu Simbel**, but this is the later Arab name meaning 'Father of the ear (of corn)' referring to the Nile Valley's agricultural prosperity. One of the distinctive features of the four huge seated figures of Rameses II is that they are wearing unusual hats shaped like containers for measuring corn. During reconstruction it was decided not to repair

A Lake Nasser cruise ship moored up at Abu Simbel

the one broken statue that collapsed during an earthquake in antiquity, so the giant torso of the second seated statue still lies at his feet.

Above the entrance door is a figure of Ra-Horakhty with a sun disc head dress. Inside the first chamber are eight columns with large Osiride figures and wall carvings of military exploits in Syria. The second pillared hall shows religious themes, with a small sanctuary of four seated figures behind this. The rebuilt temple looks fabulous, but there is a hidden secret. The 'mountain' into which the temple is slotted is actually a large empty dome with rocks stuck on the outside to make it look real. Visitors in the 1970s were invited inside the dome to view the interior, but this is no longer allowed.

Nearby is the smaller **Hathor Temple** associated with Rameses' wife Nefertari. Six standing figures look out across the lake, three on each side – the queen in the middle flanked

Abu Simbel's Illuminations

The alignment of the main Rameses II temple at Abu Simbel meant that the seated figures of the inner sanctuary were briefly illuminated by the rising sun on two days each year, 21 February and 21 October. Guides say that this was designed to celebrate the birthday and coronation of the king, but nobody is exactly sure. The phenomenon occurs because the dates are the same number of days either side of the solstices. The calculations were so precise that only three of the four figures are lit, leaving Ptah (the god associated with the underworld and death) permanently in darkness. When the temple was moved, a slight adjustment was needed to maintain this solar event. However, over the three millennia since the temple was built, the earth itself has shifted alignment and the Tropic of Cancer is now slightly further south. The three figures are still illuminated twice a year, but now on 20 February and 22 October.

The four seated figures of Rameses II at Abu Simbel

by different representations of her husband. The interior statues of the queen are finely carved and decorated with a yellow hue.

Cruise boat passengers usually have three opportunities to visit the site: once for the guided tour, another for the evening sound and light show, and again early the next morning.

LUXOR EAST BANK

Most Nile cruises lasting seven nights finish where they
started at **Luxor**, and it is now that you will have the 16
chance to explore the area's wealth of sights. East Bank sightseeing at Luxor will probably include Karnak and Luxor temples, and possibly Luxor Museum. Old hands who have been on several Nile cruises are able to miss the guided tours, free up some time and make their own

arrangements to see something different, of which there is plenty choice. Luxor mayor Samir Farag intends to turn Luxor into a 'living museum' over the next decade.

Luxor Town

A lazy afternoon or evening can be happily spent by travelling around town in a horse-drawn *calèche*. A trot along the corniche is always pleasant, perhaps on the way to the sound and light show at Karnak. The modern Luxor Souq is a lively place, which can be heaven or hell depending on your attitude to hassle and haggling. But all this chaos is left behind by taking a relaxing *felucca* trip on the Nile. An hour sailing from one side to the other gives the town a new perspective and reminds you how central the Nile is to Luxor life. Finish it off with a visit to the welcoming **Win-**

Avenue of Sphinxes

The current plan to clear away hundreds of buildings to recreate the 3km (2-mile) -long Avenue of Sphinxes between Luxor and Karnak temples is ambitious and controversial. The two temples were originally linked by the Sacred Way, and were used for an annual religious parade known as the Opet Festival during the 18th dynasty. The 1,700 sphinx statues on either side were actually added later in the 30th dynasty by Nectanebo I, most probably paid for by temple priests as they are not dedicated to any pharaohs. Less than half of the sphinxes have been recovered, as many were lost or simply disintegrated. Every museum in Egypt is now searching for any pieces that can be reconstructed, no matter how small.

The speed of the project is a concern to some archaeologists, whilst 800 families have been moved away, often with little compensation and some fine old buildings demolished. That said, when work is completed the Avenue of Sphinxes will be a remarkable sight.

ter Palace Hotel for a drink on the terrace or inside at the bar.

Winter Palace Hotel

Karnak

A temple made up of tem-
17 ples, **Karnak** (summer 6am–6.30pm, winter 6am–5.30pm; charge) is somewhat confusing for the visitor to understand, laid out as it is across such a large area. Some later temples encompassed earlier structures, which themselves were incorporated into other grand building schemes as each pharaoh tried to outdo his or her
A predecessors. The **Great Temple of Amun** essentially comprises all of the major central structures that you will see on your guided visit between the first great pylon and the inner sanctuary at the far end. As the inner sections were generally built first, you are travelling back in time as you walk from the outside towards the centre.

First is the impressive new visitors' centre, with photographs and information about the site. The approach to the entrance is quite a distance but the openness really allows the great temple pylon to be appreciated. This avenue of ram-headed sphinxes is not the one connected to Luxor Temple *(see box, left)*, but rather linked the temple to the Nile. The facade will be in shade in the morning and lit by sunlight through the afternoon. Mud ramps behind the pylon indicate that the project was suddenly abandoned and give
an idea of the construction methods involved. The **Great** B
Court is the largest of any in Egypt and contains several in-

World history

The first object in the 2010 BBC Radio 4 series *A History of the World in 100 Objects* was the inner coffin and mummy of Hornedjitef, a priest in the 3rd century BC, from the Temple of Amun at Karnak. It now lives in Room 62 of the British Museum.

teresting statues from a variety of periods, as earlier ram-headed sphinxes were pushed out of the way against the walls. On the left-hand side as you pass through the first great entrance pylon is the small **Temple of Amun, Mut and Khons**. Opposite is the entrance to the **Temple of Rameses III**, a smaller version of the entire Great Temple of Amun. Eight Osiride pillars flank its own small courtyard and there are some decent reliefs on the walls. C

Beyond the Great Court and through the second pylon is one of the highlights of any trip to Upper Egypt, the **Great Hypostyle Hall**. For millennia, visitors have marvelled at the sheer size of the 134 huge limestone columns needed to support the roof beams. The higher central columns have open papyrus flower capitals and allow daylight into the central aisle. The deep carvings are superb, said to have been ordered by Rameses II so that no later king could easily erase his cartouche. The walls are carved with the campaigns and exploits of various pharaohs, showing their might and dedication to the gods. D

E Continuing through the third pylon is the **Central Court**. Damage to the surrounding buildings opens out the whole temple, in direct contrast to the Hypostyle Hall with its maze of columns. The main point of interest here is the obelisk of Thutmose I, 23m (75ft) high and decorated with a single central band of vertical hieroglyphic text. Later texts on either side were added by Rameses IV and Rameses VI. Further still F is the **Small Hall**, noted for another famous obelisk 30m (98ft) tall and erected by Queen Hatshepsut. The twin that stood beside it has fallen and broken. The quality of the carved text on the obelisk is due to Thutmose III burying it in sand behind a walled enclosure. Look up at the obelisk to see where the colour and texture of the stone changes indicating which part was buried.

Beyond two more ruined pylons is the **Sanctuary of Sacred Barques**, built by the brother of Alexander the Great around 320BC. This small granite chapel is split into two adjoined sections – one illuminated at sunrise, the other at sunset. G

The end of the main structure is the **Festival Hall of Thutmose III** that contained the famous Table of Kings – a list of 57 earlier pharaohs that is now in the Louvre in Paris. The route continues beyond more ruined temples towards the towering Eastern Gateway alongside the giant mudbrick enclosure wall. H

Posing at Karnak's Temple of Amun

Beyond the Great Temple

Any spare time can be spent in the northern section, with its **Open Air Museum** (extra charge) – a collection of carvings, statues and small shrines. To the east of this are the Temple of Ptah and the Temple of Montu, both of which are largely in ruins and sometimes out of bounds. Beside the **Sacred Lake**, just south of the Great Temple, a large carving of a scarab beetle is said to bring good luck if you walk around it.

Running south past the lake is another series of pylons. In front of the first one is a collection of fine statues. The pylons are often out of bounds, but ultimately lead out of the compound along the eastern Avenue of Sphinxes towards the **Temple of Mut** located in front of another smaller sacred lake. A smaller, parallel access path to the west contains the Temple of Khons, best reached by passing through the Temple of Rameses III at the southern side of the Great Court. This great building and its small neighbour, the Opet Temple, were the starting point for the annual parade along the (western) Avenue of Sphinxes to Luxor Temple.

Luxor Temple

J Situated in the centre of Luxor beside the Nile, **Luxor Temple** (summer 6am–10pm, winter 6am–9pm; charge) is predominantly the work of 18th dynasty pharaohs and dedicated to the Theban triad of Amun, Mut and Khons. Amenhotep III started construction around 1500BC and Horemheb, Sety I and Rameses II added sections. The **Avenue of Sphinxes** leads to Karnak from the front of the pylon, which is decorated by two great statues of Rameses II and a single obelisk – the twin is now in Place de la Concorde in Paris. The original layout of the great court of Rameses II is interrupted by the supports for the Abu Al Haggag Mosque to the left, but still retains its intimate feel with large statues and carved walls. One of the most important scenes on the wall of the colonnade

Early air travel

In 1925, Sir Alan Cobham landed an early float-plane on the Nile at Luxor during an Imperial Airways survey between London and Cape Town. From 1932, passengers on the 12-day scheduled flying boat service to Cape Town stayed overnight at the Winter Palace Hotel.

shows details of the Opet Festival, depicting the god Amun being brought by priests along the Sacred Way to be returned by boat along the Nile.

The open court of Amenhotep III has double columns around the outside, and some of the stonework still has fine original colours. Beyond is the Hypostyle Hall, Birth Room and inner sanctuary, under whose floor a cache of royal statues was found in 1989, now displayed in Luxor Museum. You can enjoy great views of the temple from the surrounding roads – it looks particularly magnificent when illuminated at night.

Luxor Temple

For centuries after the temples had been abandoned and buried in sand, their solid roofs made ideal foundations for houses and other buildings. Archaeologists cleared these away, but one building that remained on top of the Luxor Temple was the **Abu Al Haggag Mosque**, the most important Islamic structure in Luxor. Non-Muslims can enter Abu Haggag's mausoleum and mosque if suitably dressed and having removed footwear. It is fascinating to wander around the tops of the temple columns and inspect the capitals that create the fabric of the mosque. Abu Haggag's body is placed behind the *qibla* wall, so that everyone praying towards Mecca also prays to him.

Luxor Museum

Still looking remarkably new, **Luxor Museum** (summer 9am–3pm and 5pm–10pm, winter 9am–9pm; charge; no cameras) has a a well-presented collection, explained in both English and Arabic. The five minute-introductory film is worthwhile, followed by the latest addition – the cache of 26 statues found at Luxor Temple in 1989, including a wonderful lifesize statue of Amenhotep III in smoothed and roughened dark-red quartzite. The ground floor has a series of wonderful statues, including the stunningly pristine Thutmose III made from greywacke (a hard, dark sandstone that can be worked extremely finely) and discovered at Karnak.

Luxor Museum houses a fine collection in its modern building

The **'Thebes – Glory'** section shows military details and one of King Tutankhamun's war chariots found inside his tomb. Two royal mummies are on show, including the one brought back from the Museum of Curiosities at Niagara Falls, thought to be Rameses I. A statue of Rameses II is made from a single piece of Aswan stone, with his body depicted in grey granite – yet his royal crown is of red granite. Upstairs are other items from Tutankhamun's tomb: remarkably preserved 3,000-year-old funerary papyrus, pottery, coins, unusual figures of Akenaton, mummy wrappings, and items from the Roman and Byzantine periods. Try to allow 60–90 minutes to visit this excellent museum.

A reassuring sign in Luxor

Mummification Museum

Just how the Ancient Egyptians prepared dead bodies for the journey to the afterlife is revealed through colourful tomb paintings, carvings and papyrus texts at the fascinating **Mummification Museum** (summer 9am–2pm and 5pm–10pm, winter 9am–2pm and 4pm–9pm; charge; no cameras).

Opened in 1998, it has good explanations in both English and Arabic, and subdued lighting to protect the objects. One of the main themes is the strict religious procedure that had to be followed – papyrus scrolls show Egyptian figures weighing the heart of the deceased on scales against the weight of a feather; or being absolved in front of Osiris. Parallel to this are displays on the practicalities – purifying the body; removal of the brain through the nostrils; placing vicera in four canopic jars; wrapping the mummy in resin-soaked bandages; and decoration of the body and mummy cases. There are some interesting mummies of a ram, ibis, baboon, goose, baby crocodile and some cats, as well as tomb ornaments of *ushabti* figures, scarabs and model funerary boats. Allow 30–45 minutes to do the museum justice.

Avenue of Sphinxes

Luxor Heritage Centre

Overlooking the Avenue of Sphinxes towards the Karnak end is the **Luxor Heritage Centre** (Wed–Mon 11am–8pm; tel: 095-237 3086; charge for Culturama) aimed at bridging the gap between Ancient Egypt and the modern world. It houses a library, Egyptology department, learning centre and exhibition space. The four themed zones are Culturama, 3D, Eternal Egypt and Star Riders. The purpose-built underground theatre uses nine screens to show cutting-edge **Culturama** programmes at 6pm and 7.15pm. Worth checking out is the first ever film shot in the pharaonic language, explaining the Book of the Dead with English subtitles (on Wednesday).

3D is a series of 100-year-old still images, viewed in 3D with special glasses. Alternatively, **Eternal Egypt** is a virtual tour around some of the major historical sites – a look around King Tut's tomb; Luxor Temple or the Giza plateau. **Star Riders** is a display of early Islamic navigational instruments, such as astrolabes and sundials.

Coptic Churches

Two churches on the edge of the Avenue of Sphinxes clearance zone are threatened with demolition. The twin-towered **St Mary's Church** is 180 years old and recently received relics of St Maurice in 2010. The nearby **Evangelical Presbyterian Church** is also threatened.

Al Tawd Temple and Mo'allah Tombs

Eighteen kilometres (11 miles) southwest of Luxor is the ruined but peaceful temple at **Al Tawd** (7am–6pm; ticket from Luxor Temple ticket office), dedicated to Montu, an early Theban god. Most of its stone blocks went to construct the sugar refinery across the river at Armant, but there are some fine carvings and unusual Hathor head reliefs along the tops of the walls. An avenue of sphinxes leads to a river temple once on the banks of the river.

About 40km (25 miles) south of Luxor by road are the **Mo'allah Tombs** (7am–6pm; ticket from Luxor Temple ticket office), which belonged to regional governors more than 4,000 years ago. Two are open to the public, but they do not compare well with the later Nobles' Tombs on the West Bank at Luxor or the slightly better contemporary tombs at Aswan. Tickets for both sites can only be bought at Luxor Temple ticket office beforehand. A knowledgeable taxi driver with a travel permit is your best way to reach the sites as they are not easy to locate.

Departing every Sunday from the Iberotel is the **Dandarah Temple day cruise,** heading northwards where few tourists venture. This full day on the cruise boat *Le Lotus* takes about four hours each way, passing

A Nile cruise boat

Karnak, Qus and Naqada, mooring just before the bridge at Qena. Included in the price is the coach transfer and guided tour of the quiet Ptolomaic period **temple**. Access to the roof and down into the crypt is allowed. The south wall has a carving of Queen Cleopatra. Return to the boat for lunch and the small pool and sail back to Luxor by sunset.

Day trips by coach from Luxor to Denderah also visit **Abydos temple**, centre of the cult of Osiris. This large temple of Sety I is famous for its carvings in the second Hypostyle Hall – a list of the previous 76 kings, known as the 'King's List'.

The entrance to the Valley of the Kings

LUXOR WEST BANK

Your itinerary will include the Valley of the Kings at the beginning or end of your cruise. Usually seen at the same time is Queen Hatshepsut's Temple, Colossi of Memnon and possibly one or two other tombs.

Valley of the Kings

The idea that a scorched dusty valley in Upper Egypt is one of the world's greatest tourist attractions seems unlikely. But our continuing fascination with Ancient Egypt, its pharaohs and burial tombs ensures that millions of visitors arrive each year at

the **Valley of the Kings** (summer 6am–5pm, winter 6am–4pm; charge; no cameras). The visitor's centre provides good information and has a wonderful transparent model of the valley showing the location of each tomb. A road train runs to the ticket office and entrance. A single ticket allows entry into any three of the nine tombs that are usually open; not all are open at the same time. You will need to buy an additional ticket if you want to visit **Tutankhamun's Tomb** (KV 62). It is certainly the best-known, but the interior is disappointing.

Royal cartouche

At the end of the 18th century, Napoleon's soldiers thought that the carved oval rings of hieroglyphic symbols looked like the outline of rifle cartridges, and called them *cartouche*, the French word for cartridge. At that time nobody knew that the shape contained the names of royal pharaohs.

The tombs are numbered KV (King's Valley) 1–63. Many people are happy to limit their visit to the tombs in the central area, such as those of Rameses I, VI and IX. The more adventurous can walk up to the end of the valley and clamber down to see the marvellously atmospheric unfinished **tomb of Thutmose III**, with its unusual cartouche-shaped burial chamber. All the tombs are beautifully decorated, with hieroglyphic texts and figures below star-painted ceilings to ensure the safe passage to the afterlife.

It was generally believed that all the royal tombs had been discovered, but a new one came to light in 2006 containing empty coffins (see www.kv-63.com). Further detailed information on all the tombs can be found at the excellent Theban Mapping Project site (www.thebanmappingproject.com).

Dayr Al Bahari

One of the most distinctive temples (summer 6am–5pm, winter 6am–4pm; charge) belongs to the indomitable Queen Hat-

Detail of Queen Hatshepsut's temple

shepsut, who ruled as a male pharaoh for over 20 years. The visitor's centre has a model showing her tiered temple around 1400BC. Here at **Dayr Al Bahari** (Northern Monastery) the idea of a tiered building was not new: look left to the ruined site of a similar mortuary temple, built by Mentuhotep over 500 years earlier.

Hatshepsut's temple consists of three wide facades connected by two central ramps. The middle terrace is the most interesting, with a series of bas-relief carvings on the rear walls. At the far left is the famous account of her voyage to Punt, showing trading boats carrying incense, precious woods, ivory and animal skins. You can tell it shows the Red Sea and not the Nile because the artists depicted saltwater fish below the boats. Further to the left, beyond the colonnade, is a small **Hathor temple**. The right hand colonnade shows the account of her divine birth and beyond is the Chapel of Anubis.

The upper section has recently been restored and is faced with eight figures of Osiris, some still retaining their original red colouring.

At the rear is the **Sanctuary of Amun**, possibly hiding a tunnel passing right through the mountain directly to Hatshepsut's tomb in the Valley of the Kings. There are wonderful views from this upper terrace across green fields and the Nile.

Valley of the Queens

It is quite a tough uneven 10-minute walk from the ticket office up quiet **Valley of the Queens** (summer 6am–5pm, winter 6am–4pm; charge; no cameras), where rulers buried their wives and sons. Many of the tombs are undecorated, some are painted, but none have carvings. By far the finest is that of Nefertari (wife of Rameses II), but it is not open to the public. The tombs of Prince Amenhirkopshef (son of Rameses II), Prince Khaemwaset (son of Ramses III) and Queen Teti (husband unknown) are also very fine, but the paintings are better at the nobles' and workers' tombs *(see below)*.

Tombs of the Nobles

Not only did the pharaohs wish to see themselves making it to the afterlife, but so too did many of their high-ranking officials and priests, who commissioned their own tombs on the outer fringes of the Valleys of the Kings and Queens. They chose the best artists to create more intimate tomb decorations, rather than the endless religious texts and myths of the royal tombs. The deceased is usually painted with his wife and family enjoying a bountiful life. Hunting and fishing scenes are popular, as are banquet scenes with musicians. Tickets for the **Tombs**

Queen Hatshepsut's temple at Dayr Al Bahari

of the Nobles must be purchased at the central ticket office just beyond the Colossi of Memnon and are valid for one day only. Their list indicates which sites are open (most should open 7am–5pm) and their entry fees. Entry tickets are split into groupings of two or three nearby tombs. The best grouping is the **Rekhmira** and **Sennofer** ticket, followed by the **Nakht** and **Menna** tombs. The Nakht tomb contains a famous scene of three female musicians at a banquet.

You can also buy a ticket for the **Roy** and **Shuroy** nobles' tombs in advance from the central ticket office; they are visible from Carter's house and can be visited at the same time. Visit in the morning, when the light inside these tombs is best.

Howard Carter's House

Low-domed **Howard Carter's House** (8am–5pm; free) positioned closest to the police checkpoint at the start of the

Anubis attending the body of Sennedjem, Dayr Al Madinah

road towards the Valley of the Kings was used for many years by Howard Carter, Egyptologist and discoverer of Tutankhamun's tomb, and is now restored. With 100-year-old furniture and equipment, it is an evocative time capsule, and feels as if Carter has just popped out to visit a tomb up the road.

Royal mummies

Illegal digging by local man Abd er-Rasul from Qurnah in 1871 uncovered a tomb of 40 mummies near Dayr Al Bahari. Arrested for selling a few items, he confessed and revealed the tomb's location. It was an immensely important find, including the bodies of Sety I, Rameses II and III.

Dayr Al Madinah

Tomb workers lived with their families in the village of **Dayr Al Madinah**. During the 18th and 19th dynasties,  when the pharaonic tombs were constructed, these people lived quite separately, cut off from those on the East Bank in Thebes. Excavations have revealed comfortable two-story houses in neat rows up the hillside. Most interesting are the tombs of the workers placed beneath small pyramids, giving a great insight into the lives of common people. The main religious themes are still in evidence, but there are fabulous everyday scenes too. Anubis attending the body of **Sennedjem** is one of the most famous and best preserved paintings in all Ancient Egyptian tombs. The ticket covers entry into the village and some tombs, but **Pashedo's Tomb** is a separate ticket. Both can be purchased at the central ticket office.

Al Qurnah At Tarif

Local houses have recently been cleared from the hillsides after years of confrontation between local inhabitants and the authorities. Many had been deliberately built over tombs so that the latter could be illegally excavated for generations.

Tales abound in Luxor about the inhabitants of Al Qurnah who grew wealthy on selling tomb items from their clandestine diggings, but also about the deaths following cave-ins as they dug deep underground.

Colossi of Memnon

The two enormous statues once stood in front of the mortuary temple of Amenhotep III. The right-hand statue is the so-called **Colossus of Memnon**, said to have produced strange sounds in antiquity. The upper part of the statue collapsed during an earthquake around 27BC and was partially repaired by Emperor Septimius Severus about 200 years later, after which time the sounds stopped. The temple was built too low down on the floodplain of the river, collapsing within 200 years, and the fallen blocks were used in other nearby pharaonic building projects. Almost nothing remains of the temple, but continuing excavations are unearthing re-

David Roberts

In the middle of the 19th century, Edinburgh-born artist David Roberts produced six folio volumes of 247 lithographs of Egypt, Nubia and the Holy Land. His images of huge statues and giant temples dotted with tiny human figures clambering up sandy slopes or chatting on the tops of columns are unmistakable. Even though he used a good deal of artistic licence to create a better image and balance, his precise descriptions are a valuable record of how the antiquities looked at the time: the mud houses built on the roof of Edfu Temple, interior steps descending into Esna Temple, or the Colossi of Memnon during the inundation, can no longer be seen. His drawings are so detailed that archaeologists even refer to them today, as some of the original paintwork that he recorded has disappeared. Copies of his evocative images are still seen everywhere – on postcards, prints, papyruses, tablemats and fridge magnets.

markable finds. In 2009–10 several statues were found, including a 2.5m (8ft) -high head of the pharaoh and two large statues of Thoth, god of wisdom.

Madinat Habu

If you only had time to visit one mortuary temple this would be it. With a similar layout to Karnak, **Madinat Habu** was built for Rameses III as a sprawling site full of beautifully proportioned buildings, carvings and colours. Entry is through the Ptolomaic pylon, past lion-headed Sekhmet statues. The open area before the first pylon has a small temple and chapel with a nilometer to the right. The victory carvings on the pylon are superb and beautifully highlighted in the morning sunshine. Beyond the first court is the delightful second court with its colourful carvings of gods and painted columns. Keep looking up, as some of the best preserved colours are on the underside of ceiling slabs. Much of the wall area and its explicit figure carvings were plastered over in Coptic times, luckily retaining the original reds and blues. The rear section contains the Hypostyle Hall, sanctuaries and chapels, all decorated with deep-cut hieroglyphic texts that impress at any time of the day. Make sure to walk around the out-

At the Colossi of Memnon

side of the main temple as these walls are also covered in fine carvings showing military exploits, hunting scenes and a calendar of festivals.

Rameesseum

Regular flooding has sadly ruined much of this mortuary temple for Rameses II, but its grandeur and general layout can still be seen. Often referred to as the Memnonium by early travellers, the **Ramesseum** was systematically plundered for statues and carvings. The walls are covered with the epic deeds of Rameses II, in particular the Battle of Kadesh. Remains of his giant granite statue lie collapsed beside the stairway to the court, the inspiration behind Shelley's *Ozymandias* (the Greek name for the pharaoh). Before the second court is a series of Osiride figures and the smaller head of another Rameses statue. Beyond are

The Ramesseum

the regular Hypostyle Hall and sanctuaries. Around the temple are rows of mud-arched storage rooms that held grain and food taken as taxes from the annual harvest. There are wonderful early morning views for hot air balloonists who take off from this area.

Detail of the Ramesseum

Most other mortuary temples have been destroyed but there are another two for which tickets are available. The **Merneptah temple**, near to the Ramesseum, is in poor condition, but famous as the site of the famous Israel stele, the oldest recorded mention of the state of Israel. **Sety I temple** is in better condition and located near to Howard Carter's House.

Monastery of St Theodore (Tawdros)

Off the beaten track beyond Madinat Habu, the **Monastery of St Theodore** is possibly what St Simeon's Monastery at Aswan would look like had it not been abandoned. The 25 nuns (there are no monks) claim it was built by Empress Helena, which would date it in the 4th century at the same time as St Catherine's Monastery was built in Sinai. There are some re-used carved pharaonic blocks in the walls. St Theodore is also called Al Mohareb ('the warrior') as he was a Roman soldier and a contemporary of Helena. Visitors are welcome, but do not wear shorts or revealing clothing; entry is free, but donations are welcomed. The monastery's locally produced honey is a good buy.

WHAT TO DO

Cruises to Upper Egypt usually visit sites of antiquity that require early starts. Your schedule will quickly fill up, both with historic locations and modern activities. Some trips might be included in your programme include a camel ride to St Simeon's Monastery at Aswan or *felucca* sailing at Luxor. Others, such as hot air ballooning above the West Bank, are an optional extra. What little free time there is on a Nile cruise is normally spent on the boat. It's a good idea to add a week to your itinerary to fit everything else in.

SPORTS AND OUTDOOR ACTIVITIES

Hot Air Ballooning

The ground crew will already be inflating the balloon when you arrive at 5.30am. Following a safety briefing you will clamber onboard into the basket. With a prolonged blast of the burners the craft slowly lifts off, rising above Queen Hatshepsut's mortuary temple to give fabulous views of the area's temples and tombs. Other nearby balloons add to the surreal beauty of the Nile Valley waking up at sunrise. Prevailing winds should allow you to slowly drift toward the Nile above awakening villages, lush green crops and ancient sites, whilst listening to the sounds of the villages below. Pilots judge the altitude to catch the best wind, and it is not unusual for balloons at different heights to go in different directions. If lucky, you'll get to float across the Nile, landing in fields on the eastern part of town. The chasing ground crew then help to tether the balloon and deflate it, leaving you back on the ground at 6.30am. The vast majority of

A hot air balloon lifts off over the Nile

balloon flights are operated safely with no problems, but over the years there have been one or two accidents. When this happens, all operations are closed down and new regulations and training are implemented. Check that your travel insurance covers this activity and review the safety record of the operator. Almost all balloon operators have offices off Television Street in Luxor, including:

Hod-Hod Soliman, tel: 095-237 0116; hodhodoffice@yahoo.co.uk. Established in 1993 and has an unblemished record.

Sindbad Balloons, 37 Abdel Hamed el-Omda St, Luxor, tel: 095-227 2960, 010-330 7708; fax: 095-227 5405; email: sales@sindbadballoons.com; www.sindbadballoons.com. One of the established companies. Good info and downloads on its website.

Dream Hot Air Balloons, Ahmed Shawky Street, tel and

Camel trekking is a highlight of an Egyptian holiday

fax: 095-227 5524; email: reservation@dream-balloons.com; www.dream-balloons.com.ages.

Horus Airship and Balloon, Sheraton Road, Luxor, tel: 095-228 2670; email: info@horusballoon.com; www.horus balloon.com.

Magic Horizon, Badr Street, Luxor, tel: 095-227 4060, 010-568 8439; fax: 095-227 6651; email: booking@magic horizon.com; www.magichorizon.com.

Viking Air Egypt, Ahmed Orabi St, Luxor, tel: 095-227 7212; fax: 095-227 1211; email: gm@vikingballoonsegypt.com; www.vikingballoonsegypt.com.

Camel Treks

An established camel trek takes you from Aswan's West Bank and goes to St Simeon's Monastery. There are two options for this trip. The first is to sail to the foot of the Aga Khan mausoleum and use the camel to get up and back to the distant monastery. Alternatively, sail to the Tombs of the Nobles and have the camels bring you through the desert to the monastery and then down past the mausoleum, where your *felucca* will be waiting. On the West Bank at Luxor a brand new camel terminus has been created beside Gezira Park, where safety instructions are given and camels are allocated. An hour stomping around the fields and villages is a great taste of the camel trek experience.

Donkey Treks

For many decades, tourists have used donkeys to visit the major sites on Luxor's West Bank. There is something special about following the mountain paths into the Valley of the Kings in the early morning, just as the ancient workmen did. The views across the Nile Valley and down onto the sites are superb. Shade is minimal, so an early start is needed to trot past the Colossi of Memnon, see the Valley of the Kings and gaze at Hatshepsut's Temple. A guide is needed to provide the donkeys and lead you along the correct route. The owner of the Nile Valley Hotel, Hamada Khalifa, is the best person to get information from about donkey treks.

Horse Riding

Riding a horse across the desert beyond Medinet Habu Temple on the West Bank at Luxor is a great thrill. Early morning or late afternoon are the best times, to avoid high midday temperatures. Hotel receptions or local tour companies can arrange rides, or contact **Nobi Stables** (tel: 095-231 0024), located a few minutes from the public ferry landing point on the West Bank. Helmets are provided. There are also quad bikes for hire nearby (for those less equine-inclined).

Fishing on Lake Nasser

Opened for sport fishing in 1993, there are huge specimens to be caught in the clear tranquil waters of Lake Nasser. Of the 22 types of fish in the lake, the main species of interest are Nile perch (the large 200kg specimens are generally caught during the winter months), tiger fish, catfish and tilapia. Day boat, rod hire and longer multi-day tours are available. Try **African Angler** (www.african-angler.net) or **Lake Nasser Adventures** (www.lakenasseradventure.com).

Birdwatching

Sailing is a wonderful opportunity to see local birds in their natural habitat, especially with binoculars. Spring and autumn are particularly good times to observe birds migrating between their summer breeding grounds in Europe or Asia and wintering areas in Africa. Popular sites are Kitchener Island in Aswan or Banana Island and Crocodile (now King's) Island at Luxor. Keen twitchers can expect to identify more than 100 species on a seven-day cruise. See www.osme.org.

Tenpin Bowling

One of the latest crazes in Upper Egypt is bowling. Luxor has two lanes inside the Metropolitan Bowling Club, which has a bar and sits riverside opposite the Sofitel Winter Palace Hotel. In Aswan, head along the Corniche to the new Iberotel complex with its four computerised lanes, plus pool tables.

Golf

As a sport, golf is more popular in the large Red Sea resorts, despite water shortage concerns. However, a golf course is now operating on the outskirts of Luxor. The **Royal Valley Golf Club** (tel: 095-929 0098, www.golfluxor.net) is an 18-hole course of 6,735m/yards, located a few kilometres northeast of the airport in El-Madamod District.

Fishing on Lake Nasser

Pool, Billiards and Table-Tennis

Pubs and bars have pool tables, some of which are free to use, whilst hotels have pool and billiard tables for residents. Local open-air centres in Luxor and Aswan often have table-tennis tables for anyone to use. The stillness of the Nile also means that some cruise boats even have pool tables onboard.

ENTERTAINMENT

Upper Egypt does not have a vibrant nightlife when compared with the resorts on the Red Sea or the busy city of Cairo, although at least two evenings on your Nile cruise will be taken up with organised activities. One will likely be a belly-dancing performance backed by local musicians, or a whirling dervish who spins around without getting dizzy.

You're bound to see a whirling dervish on your Nile cruise

Galabiya Party

The *Galabiya* evening will be flagged up early on your cruise so you have a chance to buy the necessary clothing. There will be opportunities to shop en route; outfits will be more expensive to purchase on the boat. For men the minimum is a long *galabiya* (traditional Egyptian garment) and some sort of headdress, either a *tarboosh* hat or a flowing headcloth. For women, the sky is the limit, with glittering dresses, sparkly shoes, bangles, necklaces, jewellery and exotic headwear. Harem pants and belly-dancing outfits are popular choices, especially if you want to win a prize. It's all an excuse for a party.

Bars and Nightclubs

Away from the cruise boats, most nightlife is centred around the larger hotels that have nightly floor shows, music and dancing *(see Recommended Hotels)*. Along Luxor's Khalid ibn el-Walid St, popular bars offer beer and live sport on TV, including:

Moulids

A *moulid* is the celebration of a holy person, rather like a saint's day. The focus for pilgrims and visitors is on the tomb, which becomes a centre for socialising and entertainment. The biggest crowds turn up for the *layla kebir* (big night) – the final night of festivities, when Sufi groups parade and dance in the streets amid frenzied activity. In Luxor, the biggest and most raucous *moulid* is that of Abu el-Haggag, celebrated two weeks before the start of the fasting month of Ramadan. Nothing in Islam encourages this, so it is probably a local Nile tradition inherited from ancient Egyptian times. The parade of small boats through the streets of Luxor probably has its roots in the sacred barque used to carry the body of the dead pharaoh.

King's Head Pub, 2nd floor above Sunrise Restaurant, tel: 095-238 0489; www.kingsheadluxor.com.

Murphy's Irish Bar, Restaurant and Basement Disco, El-Gawazat St, tel: 095-227 8112; www.murphysirishpub luxor.com. Disco 10.30pm–late.

Opposite the Hilton Hotel, beyond Karnak, is the lively **Genesis Pub** (187 Hilton Road, tel: 010-532 3323) advertising 'Dance, drink, swim and sing' with an indoor pool bar.

Sound and Light Show

Spend the evening at Karnak temple and watch the Sound and Light Show (English version at 6.30pm or 7.45pm winter, 8pm or 9.15pm summer; charge). Crowds assemble in front of the temple and are led through the complex as the narrative unfolds through Hollywood-style dialogue, orchestral accompaniment and phased lights highlighting each structure or statue. The story concludes when the audience climbs to the seating area and views the site across the sacred lake. Days and timings can vary, so check www.soundandlight.com.eg.

Within your cruise timetable there should be an opportunity to see the Sound and Light Show at Philae Temple (English versionat 6.30pm, 7.45pm or 9pm winter, 8pm, 9.15pm or 10.30pm summer; charge). The evening begins with a sunset boat ride to the island before the programme leads the guests through the temple, with actors' voices booming out the history and myths. Other sound and light shows are available at Abu Simbel and Edfu, where different languages are provided simultaneously through headphones. Abu Simbel's show is only possible for those staying overnight.

Planet and Star Gazing

A relatively new activity is to venture into the desert for an evening picnic to watch the stars and planets using high-powered telescopes. This is great on perfectly clear nights.

Try **Space Observers** (tel: 014-400 0652; email: space.observers.luxor@gmail.com) or **Space'n'Village** (tel: 010-606 0316; email: space.n.village.luxor@gmail.com).

SHOPPING

Your cruise itinerary will normally include one or two shopping opportunities at pre-selected emporiums. As long as the shopping takes second place to the historic sites, most tourists are happy to shop, and these arrangements do earn the guides and drivers valuable commissions. Luxor is the main centre for jewellery and papyrus, and the West Bank is the best place for alabaster. Aswan deals mostly with perfumes. Egyptian salesmen are experts at parting you from your money, and it's all done with a great deal of charm and hospitality.

Most cruises include shopping opportunities in the itinerary

Every cruise boat has its own small shop selling souvenirs and jewellery onboard, but the greatest choice will be at the shops near the popular hotels in Luxor. The regenerated *souqs* of Luxor and Aswan have recently been given a modern makeover, providing good pedestrianised surfaces and more display space. It is forbidden to buy or accept any antiquities; there are heavy fines at the airport if any are found in your luggage. Opposite Luxor's Isis Pyramisa Hotel is the long-established **Philippe Jewellery** (tel: 095-238 5677), a large shop with hundreds of ideas for gifts. They have another branch beside the El-Luxor Hotel, still known as the Etap (tel: 095-238 0060).

Gold and Silver

Gold has long been mined in the mountains of Egypt. A few specialist shops sell good quality gold, silver and semi-

Alabaster craftsmen at work

precious stones at prices that are reasonable compared to those in Europe. A cartouche is a bordered oblong shape containing hieroglyphic symbols of a Pharaonic name, seen carved into temple walls and columns. Your own name can be represented by hieroglyphic symbols; many of the local guides can write this for you on a piece of paper. Given a few hours, you can have this made as a uniquely Egyptian gold or silver pendant for a necklace. Towards the Luxor Sheraton are two jewellery stores, interestingly named **Lancashire Jimmy** (tel: 095-237 0022) and **Yorkshire Bob** (tel: 095-237 6590), who have been supplying gold and silver to UK visitors for many years.

Antiques and Art

Ancient Egypt and the Nile are popular subjects for paintings, carvings and sculpture in the art galleries of Luxor and Aswan. The **Abdin Art Gallery** (tel: 095-237 5869) next to the Steigenberger Nile Palace Hotel in Luxor represents many local artists who create watercolours, oils, prints and plates, many with Islamic or Coptic themes. Near the Lantern Restaurant on El-Roda el-Sharifa St is the **Nour Art Gallery and Bistro** offering 'big art, small art, modern art, traditional art, Egyptian art, jewellery, souvenirs, mosaics, paintings and graphics'. Smaller Aswan shops around the *souq* specialise in Nubian themes.

Papyrus

Every tourist shop has reams of papyri of every possible size and scene, which are a uniquely Egyptian souvenir and make great gifts. The historical skill of making papyrus was lost until Dr Ragab researched and grew papyrus along the banks of the Nile in Cairo during the 1960s. Along the corniche at Aswan is one of Dr Ragab's 'Papyrus exhibitions' (tel: 097-230 6967) selling good priced papyrus artwork.

Bargaining

Even if you don't like haggling over prices, it's all part of the buying process in Egypt. As a rule, try to settle for about half the initial price, or get something else thrown in free. It can be great fun if you don't take it too seriously.

Spices and Perfume

The base essences of almost all the international perfume brands are available at the markets in Egypt; it is considered quite a skill to outwit the salesman by requesting an obscure perfume. A range of special perfume bottles are on offer to suit every budget, all at seemingly great value. One of the most popular sections of any local *souq* are the spice sellers, where packets of quality spices and seasonings do a brisk trade. Cumin, coriander, pepper and *shatta* (ground chillies and hot peppers) are all suitable for the kitchen at a fraction of the prices you'll find back home.

Books, Prints and DVDs

Copies of David Robert's evocative prints are everywhere, showing the ancient monuments before they were cleared of sand. If you don't have room in your luggage for a big print, consider the many books, albums, folios and postcards that are available. Several good bookshops have reprinted book titles. The established bookshop Aboudy's was initially outside the Winter Palace Hotel, but has now split into two branches. The larger **Aboudy Book Store** (tel: 095-237 3390) is next to Murphy's Irish Bar down El-Gawazat St opposite the Steigenberger Nile Palace Hotel. It sells a wonderful selection of books, maps, prints and old photos. The other branch (tel: 095-237 8751) is opposite the Luxor Temple. The bookshop inside the Steigenberger Nile Palace Hotel is also good. DVDs of the sites, temples and tombs are generally good quality and are quite useful souvenirs of places where cameras are forbidden.

ACTIVITIES FOR CHILDREN

Egyptians are extremely family-orientated, so there are a number of activities that will interest younger visitors. The secret is not to do too much during the day, and to alternate sightseeing with other fun activities.

A *felucca* ride is a great way to spend a few hours, especially when the destination is Banana Island near Luxor. The boatmen are happy for children to try sailing and holding the rudder, and the trip culminates in a walk through the fruit plantations, enjoying samples along the way. Another activity children are sure to love is riding, whether it be on a camel, donkey, horse or quad bike. The excitement of riding through the fields and villages out into the desert of the West Bank at Luxor is likely to appeal to all. Rides can be arranged through your hotel or local tour operators.

Local children on board a Nile *felucca*

Animal lovers should consider visiting **Animal Care in Egypt**. This British charity's remit is to look after the welfare of working animals that are often undernourished and badly treated. The centre actively invites visitors to see the work they are doing with horses, donkeys and camels, as well as rarer local animals such as swamp cats and Egyptian tortoises. ACE (Animal Care in Egypt) is located about 10 minutes' taxi ride out of the centre on El-Habil Road, Luxor, tel: 095-928 0727; email: info@ace-egypt.org.uk; www.ace-egypt.org.uk.

If any museum is going to interest the children it is Luxor's **Mummification Museum**. It features human mummies, exposed brain cavities, funerary equipment and various mummified animals, including cats and a crocodile from Kom Ombo Temple. Luxor also has two fun public parks, the most central being at the end of St Joseph Hotel Street, with gentle rides and slides.

Luxor's Mummification Museum is full of kid-friendly exhibits

Calendar of Events

January: Coptic festival at St Theodore's Monastery, Luxor (20 January).
January/February: Egyptian International Marathon on the West Bank, starting and finishing at Queen Hatshepsut's Temple. Also half marathon, children's races and inline skating *(see www.egyptianmarathon.com).*
February: Festival of the Sun at Abu Simbel when the rising sun illuminates the statues inside the temple (22 February).
April: Sham el-Nasseem, Coptic Easter Monday *(see below).*
May: Pharaonic Wedding Festival at Karnak Temple.
June/July: Two-day Moulid of Abu el-Haggag *(see below).*
August: Celebrating the Flooding of the Nile.
October: Festival of the Sun at Abu Simbel, when the rising sun illuminates the statues inside the temple (20 October).
November: Luxor National Day and King Tut Festival celebrates the discovery on 4 November 1922 of the tomb of King Tutankhamun.
November: Pharaonic Wedding Festival at Karnak Temple.

Festivals fixed by Coptic calendar:
7 January: Coptic Christmas
19 January: Coptic Epiphany
Coptic Easter Monday is called Sham el-Nasseem (meaning 'sniffing the wind'). Families of all faiths come to public areas and parks alongside the Nile for picnics of salted fish, lupin seeds, onions and boiled eggs.
Festivals fixed by Islamic calendar:
Ashura celebration of the martyrdom of Imam Hussein on the 10th of the Islamic month of Muharram.
Moulid al-Nabi celebrates the birthday of the Prophet Mohammed.
Moulid Abu el-Haggag celebrates his birthday two weeks before the start of the Islamic month of Ramadan. From 2011 to 2013, this will take place in July.
Eid el-Fitr festival at the end of the Islamic fasting month of Ramadan.
Eid el-Adha festival to mark Ibrahim's sacrifice.
Check exact dates with tour operators as they change yearly.

EATING OUT

Egypt's location and historical influences create dishes that are a delicious combination of Lebanese, Greek, Italian, French, Turkish, Persian, Arabian, Indian and African flavours. Luxor and Aswan's proximity to Lake Nasser and the Red Sea assures a good supply of fresh fish and seafood, whilst vegetables and meat come from the Nile Valley and Delta.

All cruise boat packages include three main meals each day, usually buffet-style, and meal times are adjusted to fit around the sightseeing visits. Any pre-departure information is usually acted upon, so if you have any dietary requirements or food intolerance, let the tour company know well in advance.

Breakfast

This is usually relatively quick affairs of 30–45 minutes prior to an early site visit. The selection will include cereals, fruit salads, several types of cheeses and meats, whilst freshly baked

Ramadan

The fasting month of Ramadan affects the whole process of meal times in Egypt, but this is not a problem on a cruise boat. The majority of Egypt's population do not eat, drink or smoke through the hours of daylight, but non-Muslims are permitted to use the onboard restaurants as normal and those establishments outside that remain open. During Ramadan it is courteous not to eat, drink or smoke whilst away from the boat during the day. Beers, wines and spirits will be available on your cruise boat and in hotels. After sunset, Egyptian Muslims eat, drink and have fun throughout the night until the early morning meal, known as *suhuur*, the final meal before daylight.

breads, rolls and croissants will have just emerged from the onboard bakery. Cooked breakfasts are eggs, stuffed tomatoes, cooked meats with vegetables and peppers. A local Egyptian breakfast is *fuul* – fava beans livened up with tomatoes, onion, olive oil, cumin and other spices. Drinks will be various types of teas, coffee and fruit juices.

A friendly chef serves up dinner

Lunch

A display of substantial appetisers is on offer at lunchtime. As well as hummus, now popular around the world, you can try *tahina*, a thin paste made from ground sesame seeds with added olive oil and spices, and *babaganugh*, mashed aubergine with garlic, lemon juice and oil. A dish imported from along the North African coast is *shakshouka*, a delicious blend of chopped lamb, tomatoes, onions, herbs and spices, topped with an egg. Salads have progressed greatly from the drab offerings of a few years ago: wonderful Caesar, Greek, tuna and green salads are all prepared from high-quality local produce. Main courses will normally be fish, pasta and grilled meats.

Evening Meal

This is when the chefs can really express themselves by preparing whole fish, racks of lamb or Middle Eastern spe-

Tea and snacks on board a cruise ship

cialities, such as pigeons *(hammem)* stuffed with rice or grain. Beef, lamb or camel can be used in a *tagine* – a steaming stew of rice with onions, potatoes and tomatoes on a bed of rice or couscous, usually presented in an earthenware pot. Grilled meats will be lamb, beef or camel, together with chicken and pasta dishes.

Desserts

Most Egyptian desserts are very rich and sweet. *Om Ali* (meaning the 'mother of Ali') is a truly delicious and filling pudding, presented in a hot earthenware pot. It is made from milk, nuts, dried fruit, coconuts, cinnamon and cream, separated by layers of thin corn bread. *Baklava* is a light filo pastry stuffed with honey and nuts, whilst *kunafa* is similar but made with a more delicate shredded pastry. *Basboosa* is a semolina cake, dripping with syrup and lemon.

Drinks

Tea will be offered everywhere you go, invariably sweet, black and thick. Try to intervene beforehand if you would like it without sugar or with milk, though this is not always possible. In traditional local coffee and tea shops, coffee is thick Arabic (Turkish) or instant Nescafe.

Karkadeh is a really refreshing drink that is very popular in Upper Egypt, made from dried hibiscus blossoms served hot or cold, and originally from Nubia. A delightful way to quench a raging thirst is with a local fruit juice from one of the many colourful stands. The choice depends on what is in season, ranging throughout the year with mango, orange, watermelon, strawberry, banana, pineapple and citrus fruits. Sugar cane is grown all along the riverbank around Luxor and when crushed provides a sweet, if somewhat gritty, juice.

There are plenty of alcoholic options to choose from too. Locally produced Stella beer comes in standard, export or premium lager varieties, and the quality has risen dramatically in the past few years. Recent additions to the choices of local beers are a weaker Sakara brand and two Meister beers, of which Meister Max is the strongest. Lebanese-supervised red and white wines are also good quality, while there are Egyptian versions of the Greek *ouzo* and Lebanese *arak*, with similar aniseed flavours, to be taken neat or with ice and water, whereupon it turns milky white.

Ancient alcohol

A type of thick yeasty beer was popular in ancient Egypt and can be seen in tomb wall paintings, often represented as a form of payment to workers. Some Egyptian temples had their own vineyards to produce wine that was offered to the gods.

Restaurants

Away from your cruise boat are great specialist restaurants, especially in Luxor.

Generally the most consistent quality international food, such as Italian, Chinese or Lebanese is within the larger hotels, but a few independent restaurants are very good. Non-residents can use hotel restaurants and you might need to observe a dress code at the Sofitel Winter Palace and Sonesta St George in Luxor, or Sofitel Cataract Hotel in Aswan. Almost all restaurants serve local beer and wine.

Smoking a *sheesha* (or hubble-bubble) water pipe is becoming more common in local restaurants and cafés. The tobacco itself is usually thick and pungent, often mixed with other flavours such as apple or molasses.

MENU READER

apple	toofa	**olives**	zaytoon
aubergine	berinjan	**onions**	bassal
beans	fuul	**oranges**	burtogaan
beer	beera	**pasta**	makaruna
bread	aysh	**pepper**	filfil
butter	zubda	**pineapple**	ananas
cheese	jibda	**potatoes**	batatas
chicken	frakh	**prawns/ shrimps**	gambari
chickpeas	hummus		
chocolate	shokolata	**rice**	ruz
coffee	ahwa	**salad**	salata
eggs	beerd	**salt**	melh
fish	samak	**soup**	shorba
liver	kibda	**sugar**	sukkar
meat	lakhma	**tea**	shai
without meat	bidoon lakhma	**tomatoes**	tamatum
		vinegar	khall
meatballs	kufta	**water**	moyya
milk	laban, haleeb	**watermelon**	bakhteerkh
		wine	nabeet
mushrooms	shampinyon	**the bill**	fattoura

PLACES TO EAT

We have used the following symbols to give an idea of the price for a two-course meal for one person, including a glass of wine:

££££ over £50	££ £5–25
£££ £25–50	£ under £5

LUXOR

1886 ££££ *Winter Palace Hotel, Corniche An Nil, East Bank; tel: 012-238 0422; daily 7pm–midnight.* The Winter Palace's flagship restaurant, 1886 has long reigned as Luxor's top table. The restaurant has a dress code of jacket and tie, and the service in the rarefied dining room is formal and attentive. French-style with Egyptian influence and ingredients, the cuisine is creative and sumptuous, though the mark-up on the wine list is very steep.

African Garden Restaurant £–££ *Al Gezira, West Bank; tel: 012-365 8722; daily 10am–11pm.* Located around 100m/yds straight up from the ferry terminal, the African's biggest plus is its large, verdant and shaded terrace. Prices have increased recently, and the food is good but not outstanding, but the three-course local-style lunch and dinner for LE30 is good value. Pizzas, pasta, soups and salads also feature on the menu.

Al Moudira ££–£££ *Al Moudira Hotel, Daba'iyya, West Bank (10km/6 miles south of the Valley of the Queens); tel: 012-325 1307; daily 7am–10.30pm.* The Moudira offers imaginative, well-presented and beautifully cooked European-Middle Eastern fusion cooking. The service is impeccable, and the atmosphere intimate, romantic and tranquil. It's the perfect place for dinner *à deux*.

Bombay Restaurant ££ *Shari' Khaled Ibn Al Walid, East Bank (near the Sheraton Hotel); tel: 012-238 7935; daily noon–midnight.* The Bombay Restaurant offers classic curries with all the usual trimmings, including naan breads, poppadoms and samosas. It's a great choice for vegetarians, and prices are reasonable.

Miyako Restaurant £££ *Sonesta St George Hotel, Shari' Khaled Ibn Al Walid, East Bank; tel: 012-238 2575; daily noon–11pm.* Popular in particular for its *teppanyaki* prepared by chefs in front of you, cool, low-lit and peaceful Miyako also offers reasonable sushi, sashimi and sake.

Oasis Cafe £–££ *Shari' Dr Labib Habashi, East Bank; tel: 095-336 7121; daily 10am–10pm.* Occupying a renovated 1930s house in the centre of town, this café-cum-restaurant serves decent coffee and a good range of international dishes in peaceful and laid-back surroundings, often to the tunes of jazz or Sufi music.

Snobs £–££ *Off Shari' Khaled Ibn Al Walid, East Bank (near Sonesta Hotel); tel: 012-236 0356; daily noon–midnight.* Snobs restaurant serves fresh, well-cooked and slightly more imaginative Western fare than is the average in Egypt. Pizza, pasta, salads, soups and steaks are home-made and reasonably priced. Representing good value, it's also well managed and friendly.

Sofra £–££ *90 Shari' Muhammad Farid, behind the Old Winter Palace, East Bank; tel: 095-235 9752; daily 11am–midnight.* With its diminutive dining rooms and funky decor, Sofra is a quirky, intimate and friendly little place, serving fresh Egyptian food at excellent prices. There's also a lovely roof terrace. No alcohol is served, but there's a good selection of fresh fruit juice.

Tutankhamun £ *200m/yds south of the ferry landing; West Bank; tel: 012-231 0918; daily noon–11pm.* This simple, rustic Egyptian restaurant's biggest asset is its roof terrace, which affords fantastic Nile views. Mahmoud, the patron, is renowned for his home-made *tagens* (casseroles cooked in clay pots and then baked in the oven). The rosemary chicken served with oriental rice is famous.

ASWAN

1902 Restaurant £££–££££ *Sofitel Old Cataract Hotel, Shari' Abtal At Tahrir; East Bank; tel: 097-231 6000; daily noon–11pm.* The Old Cataract's pride and joy, and the top restaurant in town, 1902 is currently undergoing a major facelift. When it reopens (billed for May 2011), it should reintroduce its fine formula of French-meets-Levantine cuisine served up in the grand dining room. European wines are available, but the mark-up is astronomical.

Al Masry £ *Shari' Al Matar; East Bank; tel: 097-230 2576; daily noon–midnight.* The decor might be slightly Orientalist-kitsch, but Al Masry claims to do the best kebabs and *kofta* in town, along with succulent and tasty chicken and sometimes pigeon and quail. Sold by weight or size, cooked to perfection and served in large portions with lashings of tahini, *khobz* (bread) and salad, it's a great place to come for first-rate local food at unbeatable prices.

Aswan Moon £–££ *Corniche An Nil, East Bank; tel: 097-231 6108; daily 11am–midnight.* The town's most famous floating restaurant, the Aswan Moon boasts a great setting, friendly service and a lively atmosphere. In high season, entertainment is usually staged nightly. The food (Levantine favourites such as kebabs and roast chicken) is variable, but it's the ambience that you come for.

Koshary Ali Baba Restaurant £ *Shari' Abtal At Tahrir, East Bank; no tel; daily 10am–midnight.* It may not look like much, but Ali Baba is considered the town's top *koshari* joint. Simple and clean, it's a great place to come to try Egypt's famous, carb-heavy dish, though prices do tend to rise for tourists.

Koshary El-Zaeem £ *Meadan Hussain, East Bank; daily 24hrs.* With a fervent local following, Koshary El-Zaeem is considered one of Aswan's best *koshari* joints. Hearty portions are topped with generous amounts of spicy tomato sauce and fried onion. Most people opt for takeaway, but you can sit and eat at one of the dusty tables if you can find one that's free.

Panorama £ *Corniche An Nil, East Bank; tel: 097-231 6169; daily 10am–midnight.* Situated opposite the Hanafi Souq, the Panorama is well named, with a pleasant and cool terrace overlooking the river. With its menu of fresh fruit and herb juices (including *karkadeh* – hibiscus) and simple but delicious meat and vegetable dishes (*mezzes* and mains), it's a great place to come for honest Egyptian home cooking.

A–Z TRAVEL TIPS

A Summary of Practical Information

A

ACCOMMODATION *(see also list of RECOMMENDED HOTELS and CRUISE BOAT OPERATORS)*

Accommodation on Nile cruise holidays is always onboard the boat. If extending your stay, there is a range of quality hotels stretching along the Nile south of Luxor centre, with smaller hotels over on the West Bank. Aswan is limited in its choice of hotels. Walk-in rates at hotels can be very expensive, so book online or through a tour operator for the best deals. Most hotels can be paid for with credit cards, but some of the smaller places will only accept cash.

hotel	fondu
how much?	bi kam?

AIRPORT

The international airport at Luxor (code LXR) was upgraded in 2005. Exchange banks and entry visa purchases are before immigration, with ATM bank machines outside. Transfer to the cruise boat takes around 15–25 minutes depending on where the boat is moored. When departing, surplus Egyptian pounds can be spent after passport control. There is no departure tax.

Aswan is a smaller international airport (code ASW), mainly handling EgyptAir flights to and from Cairo, plus the daily sightseeing flights down to Abu Simbel. The Luxor and Aswan airports are still military bases where photography is prohibited.

B

BICYCLE HIRE

Free time in Luxor can be spent cycling to the various sites, and is especially pleasant on the West Bank. Due to the heat at midday, early starts are best. For the West Bank, plan your day in advance, as some entry tickets are purchased from a central ticket office located just beyond the Colossi of Memnon. The narrow roads up to the Valley of the Kings and Queen Hatshepsut's Temple are busy and should not be used by cyclists. When riding back from the sites, take the smaller roads and tracks through the villages to avoid the danger of traffic.

Behind the West Bank public ferry landing are a few bicycle rental shops, such as Mohammed Setouhy (tel: 095-231 2906, mobile: 010-223 9710). Most owners speak English, and can give advice on routes, sites and tickets as well as provide locks for securing the bikes. Check the bicycle thoroughly beforehand – especially brakes and tyres – and be aware that most bicycles are hired without helmets and are not well maintained. Hire rates are US$3–4 per day.

BUDGETING FOR YOUR TRIP

Most Nile cruise packages include flights, transfers, three/four/seven nights on a cruise boat and sightseeing tours. Check exactly what is included in your cruise package, as some sightseeing tours might cost extra. Not usually included are tips for boat crew and guides *(see page 119)*, drinks (unless all-inclusive), laundry and optional sightseeing. The following prices in LE (Egyptian Pounds) and US$ will give a rough idea of how much you will spend.

Airport transfer. From Luxor international airport to the centre of town or cruise boat mooring, US$20.

Guides. Site guide for a half day tour, US$30.

Hotels. If extending your cruise, this could be your largest expense, costing US$20–400 per night *(see Recommended Hotels, page 139)*.

Internet. 5–10LE per hour in local internet café, 10–25LE in a hotel or on a cruise boat.

Meals and drinks. Most cruises provide three good meals a day. Alcoholic, soft drinks and water are expensive onboard, so maybe choose an all-inclusive package. Set menu or buffet lunch/dinner in a two/three-star hotel or local restaurant 40–80LE, in four/five-star

hotel 100–250LE. Evening meal in downtown restaurant, 50–150LE. Soft drink/coffee in café, 5–10LE. Bottle of Egyptian beer, 12–30LE. Bottle of Egyptian wine, 75–180LE.
Sightseeing. Admission to sites and museums, 25–80LE per visit.
Taxis. Trip from central Luxor or Aswan to cruise boat moorings, 20–30LE. Horsedrawn *calèche* from central Luxor to Karnak Temple, 25–40LE.

C

CLIMATE

Upper Egypt is a desert region; there are only two main seasons – a mild winter and a hot summer. Temperatures throughout the year in Luxor average between 14 and 33°C (57 and 92°F) but can climb to more than 45°C (113°F) on some days in June, July and August. It gets hotter further south towards Aswan and Sudan. Rainstorms are very unusual and it might not rain for many years. The following chart gives the average monthly temperatures in Luxor:

	J	F	M	A	M	J	J	A	S	O	N	D
°C	14	16	19	26	30	32	33	32	30	26	21	16
°F	57	61	66	79	86	90	92	90	86	79	70	61

CLOTHING

Loose-fitting clothes made from natural fibres are the best for winter daytime and summer when temperatures get uncomfortably hot. Swimwear is only acceptable on boat sundecks and around hotel pools. Topless bathing is illegal everywhere in Egypt. Tourists are expected to dress properly within the boat restaurant areas. Dress conservatively when visiting the ancient sites and local areas. Always carry a sunhat, high factor suncream and sunglasses. In winter a jacket is useful, as are layers of clothing to keep warm, especially at night on the river.

Bring comfortable walking shoes for extensive sites such as Karnak Temple and the Valley of the Kings. Some top cruise boats and hotels have dress codes for their restaurants.

CRIME AND SAFETY

The main concern is occasional pick-pocketing and theft. Take the same precautions as at home. If anything is stolen, report it immediately to a police station and obtain a report for insurance purposes. There are always plenty of Tourist Police around the main sites to help if you have any difficulty *(see page 117)*.

Egypt has suffered from terrorism in the past, but there have been no serious attacks on tourists in Upper Egypt for more than a decade. The authorities will have security checks on all cruise boats, hotels and tourist sites. Wherever you go, you will see security policemen and armed guards whose sole purpose is to protect you. Considering the sheer number of visitors in Upper Egypt every year, there are surprisingly few problems.

E

ELECTRICITY

Egypt uses 220V–240V/50Hz current, so most European appliances will be fine. Sockets are mainly standard Continental European round two-pin plugs. Electricity supply is assured on all cruise boats and is reliable in hotels. US goods on 110v will need a transformer.

EMBASSIES, CONSULATES AND HIGH COMMISSIONS

The embassies are in all in Cairo:

Australia: World Trade Centre, 11th Floor, Corniche el-Nil, Bulak, Cairo; tel: 02-2570 2975.

Canada: 26 Kamel el-Shenawy St, Garden City, Cairo; tel: 02-2794 3110; email: cairo@dfait-maeci.gc.ca.

Ireland: 3 Abu el-Feda St, Zamalek, Cairo; tel: 02-2340 8264/8547.

South Africa: 21/23 Giza St, 18th Floor, Giza.
UK: 7 Ahmed Ragheb St, Garden City, Cairo; tel: 02-2794 0852/0/8; www.britishembassy.org.eg. The consular section can be contacted by tel: 02-2791 6000, Sun–Thur 9am–2pm, and opens for personal callers 9.30am–1.30pm except holidays.
US: 5 Latin America St, Garden City, Cairo; tel: 02-2797 3300.

EMERGENCIES

Report any emergency to the nearest Tourist Police, security officer or army personnel. Emergency telephone numbers are:
Police: **122**
Tourist Police: **126**
Ambulance: **123**
Fire: **125**

G

GAY AND LESBIAN TRAVELLERS

Homosexuality is technically illegal in Egypt, but some couples do have same-sex relationships and certain nightclubs and bars are gay hang-outs. Gay and lesbian visitors will have few problems as long as they are discreet and cautious. Local men often greet other with kisses and hold hands, but this is not the sign of a gay relationship.

GETTING THERE *(see also TOURIST INFORMATION)*

By air. From the UK the main charter carriers flying once a week to Luxor are Monarch (London Gatwick and Manchester); Thomson (London Gatwick, Birmingham, Manchester and Bristol); and Thomas Cook (London Gatwick, Birmingham and Manchester). Easyjet fly twice-weekly from London Gatwick. EgyptAir fly daily scheduled flights to Luxor from London Heathrow. There are no direct flights from the UK to Aswan. Some European airlines fly weekly to Luxor including Austrian Airways and Lauda Air (Austria);

Transavia (France); Air Berlin (Germany). Middle Eastern airlines include Qatar Airways, Air Arabia and Kuwait Airways. Many other airlines fly into Cairo, from where the national carrier EgyptAir can connect to Luxor or Aswan; www.egyptair.com.eg.

By train. Between Cairo and Upper Egypt, overnight sleepers are operated by Abele Egypt (www.sleepingtrains.com); usually with three trains daily each way. Trains leave Cairo at 8pm, 8.30pm (originates from Alexandria at 5.20pm) and 9.10pm, taking about nine hours to Luxor and 12 hours to Aswan. Trains depart Aswan at 5pm (goes on to Alexandria), 6.30pm and 9.20pm, all stopping at Luxor around three hours later. Tickets cannot be booked on the website, only at the main railway ticket offices in Cairo, Luxor and Aswan or through travel agencies *(see Guides and Tours, below)*. Day trains are usually very slow and foreign tourists might not be allowed to use them for security reasons.

By road. Until recently access to Luxor and Aswan by road from elsewhere in Egypt was subject to strict controls via a series of daily convoys. These restrictions have been lifted and it is now possible to travel to and from Cairo along the Nile Valley, and to and from Hurghada on the Red Sea. Vehicles that still need permission should make arrangements the day before. However, any security incident or threat could reinstate the convoy system at any time. Special permission and security arrangements are required to travel across the Egyptian/Sudanese road border south of Abu Simbel.

By boat. A weekly ferry sails each way between Aswan and Wadi Halfa in Sudan. The overnight journey takes around 18 hours and sails past all the rescued temples (including Abu Simbel), but some of these will be passed at night. Arriving from Sudan, all Egyptian entry formalities and visa purchases are completed on the ferry and at Aswan.

GUIDES AND TOURS

Sightseeing excursions from the cruise boat are normally included in your tour package. If booked with an agent inside Egypt they might not be, so always check. Extra guided tours can be added if there is time before or after your cruise. Local tour agencies can provide transport and a guide for any number of days. Many tour companies have their own cruise boats. Others recommended are:

Memphis Tours, 1st Yehia el-Bahnasawy, off Hospital St, Luxor, tel: 095-228 2662, 010-733 2151, www.memphistours.net.

Misr Global Travel, Corniche el-Nil St, Luxor, tel: 095-238 0951, 095-237 3551; Tourist Centre, Aswan, tel: 097-231 3400/1, www.misrtravel.net.

Nobles Tours, Corniche el-Nil St, Luxor, tel: 010-089 0111, www.noblestours.com

Several tour offices offering daily excursions and longer tours are located outside the Winter Palace Hotel in Luxor, including:

Abu Simbel Travel, tel: 095-237 2470, 010-166 4548.

American Express Travel Services, Winter Palace Building, tel: 095-237 8333, email: luxor@amexfranchise.com.

Carlson Wagonlit Travel, tel: 095-237 2317, 011-850 6007.

Jolley's Travel, tel: 095-237 2262, 010-508 7951.

Karnak Travel, tel: 095-237 2360, 010-608 2816.

Sunrise Tours, tel: 095-237 7776, 010-094 8496.

Thomas Cook, Winter Palace Building, tel: 095-237 2402; email: tcluxor@thomascook.com.eg; www.thomascookegypt.com.

Lake Nasser Adventure, tel: 012-104 0255; fax: 097-232 3636; www.lakenasseradventure.com. Sport fishing, desert adventures, trekking, wildlife tours and cruises.

H

HEALTH AND MEDICAL CARE

Most tourist illnesses are temporary. Stomach upsets are the most common, often due to poor hygiene, unclean water or the change of environment. Too much sun can cause also problems, so cover up and drink plenty of water (tap water on cruise boats and in hotels is fine for brushing teeth, but tourists should drink bottled water, available everywhere). Avoid food that is not freshly cooked or has been lying around for a long time. Full health insurance is recommended.

Vaccinations. None are compulsory, but are recommended for polio, tetanus, typhoid and hepatitis A. Check at www.mdtravelhealth.com.

For less serious ailments, modern pharmacies in every town can give professional advice and medicines. Cruise boats can always call for an English-speaking doctor or locate the nearest open pharmacy. There are two hospitals in Luxor that must be paid for in cash, with costs being reclaimed from your travel insurer. For more serious medical care, put the insurance company in direct contact with the hospital. Hospitals in Upper Egypt are limited in their facilities but are the initial point of contact for any accidents. For an ambulance call 123.

International Hospital Luxor, Hospital St (Sharia Mustashfa), tel: 095-238 7194/3/2.

Luxor General Hospital, along the Corniche just north of Luxor Museum, tel: 095-237 2025/2809.

Aswan Teaching Hospital, tel: 097-230 5311.

Evangelical Mission Hospital, Aswan, near the Corniche, tel: 097-231 7176.

Mubarak Military Hospital, Aswan, near Nubia Museum, tel: 097-231 7985.

Help me!	**Il ha ooni**
Call a doctor	**ayzin doktor**

L

LANGUAGE

Arabic is the official language. Egyptian Arabic is widely used throughout the Arab world due to the popularity of Egyptian television, cinema and music. English will be understood on the cruise boats and many locals dealing with tourists speak several European languages. Trying a few words of Arabic is appreciated by the locals. Some useful Arabic words and phrases:

yes/no	**aywa/la**
hello	**salam aleykum**
(response to hello)	**aleykum salam**
hello/welcome	**ahlan wa sahlan**
OK	**tamam, maashi**
please	**min fadlak**
thank you	**shukran**
(response to thank you)	**afwan**
how are you?	**izayak?**
I am fine	**al humdillilah**
good morning	**sabah al-kher**
good evening	**mesa al-kher**
goodbye	**ma'a salama**
what is your name?	**izmak eh?**
my name is	**izmi ...**
I do not understand	**ana mush fahem**
do you speak English?	**inta bititkalem inglizi?**
market	**souq**
mosque	**jama**

MAPS

Sadly the quality of maps is not great for the main tourist sites in Upper Egypt. Aboudy Book Stores in Luxor produce their own maps of Luxor and Aswan. There is good detail in the Kümmerley and Frey *Egypt* (scale 1:950,000), showing the original and new positions of the rescued temples along Lake Nasser. The same map is also printed in Egypt by Lehnert and Landrock, available in some souvenir and bookshops. The Insight FlexiMap of Egypt (scale 1:930,000), has a plan of Luxor and ancient sites, is double-sided and laminated.

MEDIA

Newspapers. The *Egyptian Gazette* (www.egyptiangazette.net.eg), established in 1880, is published daily and is sometimes for sale in Luxor and Aswan. Published every Thursday is *Al Ahram Weekly* (http://weekly. ahram.org.eg), an English-language version of the state-owned Arabic newspaper *Al Ahram*. *Egypt Today* magazine is popular; www.egypttoday.com. The new *Luxor Times* magazine covers stories of local interest for ex-pats and tourists; www.luxortimes.com.
Television and radio. Channels 1 and 2 are national, with English news nightly on Channel 2. Channel 3 is the Cairo channel, with Nile TV and Dream TV providing imported English programmes. All cruise boats and hotels have satellite TV offering greater choice from overseas including BBC Worldwide and CNN. On the radio is the BBC World Service, and English news can be found at FM95.

MONEY

The Egyptian pound (LE) has been tied to the US dollar for many years and fluctuates accordingly. There are Egyptian currency notes for 200LE, 100LE, 50LE, 20LE, 10LE, 5LE and 1 LE, 50 and 25 piastres (100 piastres = 1LE). There are new 1LE coins.

The local economy operates on cash, and away from the boat you should do the same. Bring US dollars, Euros or Sterling cash and exchange money at the airport as it can be difficult to do so onboard. There are many ATMs in Luxor and Aswan, and money exchanges open every day 8am–10pm. When exchanging money insist on small denominations, as there is never enough small change.

Cruise drinks and extras can be paid for by credit card. Traveller's cheques are now a real hassle to change and attract large commissions.

O

OPENING HOURS

Banks. 8.30am to 2pm, closed Friday, Saturday and most holidays.
Business. 8am to 4 or 5pm, closed Friday, some closed Saturday, and most holidays.
Government offices. 8am to 3pm, closed Friday and most holidays.
Shops. Daily 9am to 10pm in summer (10am to 9pm in winter). Some closed Sunday.

P

POLICE

Two armed policemen will be on your boat the entire time. There is a bewildering assortment of uniformed guards, police and army personnel on duty, mainly for your safety. Any tourist in need of help will usually be attended to by an English-speaking officer. Tourist Police are generally helpful, especially those in offices at the airports. Reporting a crime can be time-consuming due to the paperwork involved, but you will always be courteously processed through the system.

POST OFFICES

The postal system generally works very well. Stamps can be bought from your boat reception, hotels, post offices and some shops. Most post offices open daily 8.30am–3pm, except Friday and some holidays. The main post office in Luxor is opposite Luxor Temple, at the start of El-Mahatta Street leading to the railway station. Allow five days for airmail to Europe and up to two weeks to the USA.

PUBLIC HOLIDAYS

There are two types of official holidays when government offices and banks are closed, secular (fixed) and religious (variable dates). Islamic dates move forward roughly 11 days every year with the

Islamic calendar. The fixed holidays are:

7 January	Coptic Christmas
22 February	Union Day
25 April	Sinai Liberation Day
1 May	Labour Day
18 June	Evacuation Day
1 July	Bank Holiday
23 July	Revolution Day
11 September	Coptic New Year
6 October	Armed Forces Day
23 October	National Liberation Day
24 October	Suez Victory Day
23 December	Victory Day

Egypt's variable holidays which change with the Islamic calendar are:

Fatih Muharram	Islamic New Year
Ashura Day	commemorates the martyrdom of Hussein ibn Ali
Eid el-Fitr	(The Minor Feast) celebrates the end of Ramadan for three days
Eid el-Adha	(The Grand Feast) commemorates the sacrifice of Abraham

R

RELIGION

Tourists wishing to visit any mosques, such as Abu el-Haggag at Luxor Temple, should remove their shoes and avoid entering during Friday midday prayers, the holiest time of the week.

T

TELEPHONES

The international code for Egypt is +20. The local code for Luxor and Esna is 095, for Aswan, Abu Simbel, Kom Ombo and Edfu is

097. To call other cities in Egypt use the following codes:

Alexandria	03
Cairo	02
Hurghada	065

Most cruise boats and hotels offer direct dial services from your cabin or room, but this can be expensive.

Mobile phones. Bring your own phone, as the three major operators (Vodafone, Mobinil and Etisalat) have their own networks and agreements. If you intend using your mobile a lot, consider buying a cheap local SIM card for better rates on internal and international calls.

TIME ZONES

Egypt is two hours ahead of GMT, and there is summer daylight savings (making it one hour ahead of GMT) from late April to late September. Without any adjustments:

New York	London	Egypt	Sydney	Auckland
5am	10am	noon	7pm	9pm

TIPPING

On cruise boats it is customary to tip the crew as a whole, covering kitchen staff, waiters, reception, crew, engineers and cabin cleaners. Guidelines for the amounts will be given to you by your tour manager, but think along the lines of US$30 per tourist for a seven-night cruise. The tour rep will also need to tip the bus drivers, site guards etc with an additional US$15 per person, and then the tour manager/rep/guide themself will need another US$15. These extra amounts are not normally included in the initial cost of the holiday and should be paid at the end of your cruise.

Away from the boat everyone will want a tip. Taxi drivers, ticket sellers and site attendants all ask for *baksheesh*. These relatively small tips in western terms are useful boosts to low family incomes.

TOURIST INFORMATION

Luxor's main Tourist Office is opposite the railway station, with a smaller one inside the station and another along the Corniche in front of the Winter Palace Hotel. In Aswan the very helpful main Tourist Office is slightly hidden away near the Marhaba Palace Hotel, not far from the railway station, with another small office immediately outside the station.

There are many Egyptian Tourist Offices worldwide:
Canada: 1253 McGill College Ave, Suite 250, Montreal, H3B 2Y5; tel: (514) 861 4420, (514) 861 8071; email: eta@total.net
South Africa: First Floor, Regent Place Building, Mutal Gardens, Gradock Avenue, Rosebank, Johannesburg; tel: 002711 880 9602/3 002711 880 9604
UK: Egyptian House, 170 Piccadilly, London W1V 9DD; tel: 0207 493 5282/3, 0207 408 0295; email: tourismegypt@visitegypt.org.uk
US: 630 Fifth Ave, Suite 1706, New York, NY 10111; tel: (212) 332 2570, (212) 956 6439; email egyptoursp@aol.com

TRANSPORT

Taxis. Away from the cruise boat and its guided tours, it is best to use an official taxi. Get local advice on fares and always fix the price before getting in. If you find a good taxi driver who speaks some English, pay them to wait for you, or maybe hire them for a few hours. Taxis need permits to take foreign tourists out of Luxor or Aswan.
Buses. Daily buses run up and down the Nile Valley to Cairo and also to the Red Sea coast. Prices are good value, but timetables can be unreliable and bus stations are often on the outskirts of towns. Currently there are no restrictions on buses having to travel in police convoys.
Trains. Several slow local trains run between Luxor and Aswan, with stops at Esna and Edfu. Buy tickets an hour beforehand at the station, or on the train itself. Depending upon the security situation, tourists might not be allowed to travel on local trains. For overnight sleepers, see *Getting to Upper Egypt, page 111*.

Ferries. The public Nile ferry is an easy and cheap way to get to the West Bank in Luxor, departing around every 15 minutes outside Luxor Temple. Small motor launches are always nearby if needed. In Aswan a ferry leaves from outside the EgyptAir office for Elephantine Island.
Calèches. Traditionally the way to get around Luxor and Aswan. It's a pleasant ride out to Karnak Temple from Luxor. Bargain hard, fix the price and check the condition of the horse before getting in.
***Felucca* rental.** *Felucca* boatmen are all along the corniches of Luxor and Aswan. Agree the cost exactly (and in which currency) and the itinerary, such as going up to Banana Island (nominal entry fee) from Luxor or across to Kitchener's Island (entry fee) at Aswan. Bargain on US$10 per hour for two to three hours in the late afternoon.

TRAVELLERS WITH DISABILITIES

The *Amarco I* operated by Optima Cruises (www.optimacruises.com) has four cabins adapted for wheelchair use, with grab bars, roll-in showers and wider doorways for easier access. Some of the newer cruise boats have lifts between decks; otherwise the stairs are a problem. Getting on and off the boat along gangways is also not easy, especially if moored on the outside of several boats, but there are always plenty of friendly staff to help. Memphis Tours can put a package together (www.memphistours.com).

Away from the boat there have been great improvements, with ramps now at some of the sites and new museums, but there are still plenty of ancient steps and huge roadside kerbs to negotiate.

V

VISAS AND ENTRY REQUIREMENTS

Tourist and business visas are required to enter Egypt for all nationalities (except other Arab countries) and passports must be valid for a minimum of six months. The easiest and cheapest way to buy a tourist visa is upon arrival – you don't even need a photograph. Single- and multiple-entry visas may be obtained beforehand from an Egyptian Embassy or through a specialist visa company. Up to date information can be obtained from any tour operator, tour agency or visa specialist such as Travcour (www.travcour.com) and www.traveldocs.com. Also check www.touregypt.net/usconsulates.htm.

Passports are required at your cruise boat or hotel reception upon arrival, when they take a photocopy. If you are staying for longer than one month, visa extensions can be obtained in Luxor. Most items of tourist baggage are allowed into Egypt without any problem, but laptops and some digital equipment might be recorded in your passport to ensure they leave when you do. There is a duty-free shop upon arrival at Luxor international airport with a personal allowance of one litre of spirits and two cartons of cigarettes. A maximum of 5,000LE can be carried in or out of the country.

W

WEBSITES AND INTERNET CAFÉS

Some boats offer Wi-fi or computers with Internet access for rent. Downtown areas have Internet cafes, with Wi-fi connections at a few coffee shops and some hotels. Rates per hour vary greatly.

General tourist information websites include:

www.touregypt.net and **www.egypt.travel** – Ministry of Tourism
www.eternalegypt.org
www.al-bab.com/arab/countries/egypt.htm
www.travellersinegypt.org
www.sis.gov.eg – Egyptian State Information Service

Websites about the Upper Egypt region:

www.luxoregypt.org – useful info and a street map of Luxor town
www.luxor4u.com
www.luxortraveltips.com
www.modernluxor.com
www.topix.com/eg/luxor

CRUISE BOATS & OPERATORS

No list of boats and operators crusing the Nile will ever be complete, as boats are regularly taken out of service for upgrade, whilst others lie dormant during the slack summer period and new boats are continually being introduced. Details of each boat are available on the operator's website, which should provide deck plans, cabin layouts, details of facilities and photographs. Some show registration certificates and safety approvals, such as the international Crystal Certificate for health standards. Some also give departure days with schedules and itineraries. Check if they are linked with any major international tour operators. Larger operators have up to 20 boats, others just a single vessel – in which case the website is often the name of the boat.

The five-star rating issued by the Egyptian authorities is somewhat misleading, as it covers around 90 percent of the boats in service, and is split into various sub-categories by the boat operators themselves, such as five-star luxury plus, five-star deluxe, five-star premium and five-star standard. There can be quite a gap between five-star luxury and five-star standard. A higher classification of NN (New Norm) currently applies to just three boats (*Oberoi Zahra*, *Marco II* and *Concerto*), but this will increase as boats are refurbished and updated.

Most of the boats consist of five decks, unless indicated, with the majority of boats laid out in the same way:

Deck 1 is the lowest deck to the water line, and used for the main restaurant and kitchen.

Deck 2 has the reception, lobby and some cabins.

Deck 3 has mainly cabins.

Deck 4 has mainly cabins and the captain's bridge.

Deck 5 is usually a full-length sundeck with loungers, plunge pool, bar and awnings to provide shade.

Boat ownership is not obvious, as many are leased to international tour companies who advertise their name on board.

Below is an alphabetical list of operators, with the vessels they run. The number in brackets after the boat name is the total number of cabins (or suites) onboard. The difference between cabins and suites is also uncertain, and seems to be left to the individual operator to decide. Suites are generally larger, better positioned (on a higher deck, or with a forward-facing view), have more gadgets and fittings, windows that open or possibly a small balcony. Unless otherwise stated, boats are five-star rated.

MAJOR OPERATORS

ABERCROMBIE & KENT www.akegypt.com
Small, sleek luxury boats in gold and white colours.
Nile Adventurer (34)
Sun Boat III (22)
Sun Boat IV (42)
Sun Boat I (21, ***)
AL AHLIA NILE CRUISES www.alahlianilecruises.com
Premium (56 plus 4 suites), cream and white trim.
AMARCO NILE CRUISES www.amarconilecruise.com
Amarco II (35 suites), new boat classed NN.
ANGELOTEL NILE CRUISES www.angelotel.com
Etoile Du Nil III (45), also known as *Le Scribe.*
Etoile Du Nil II (51), also known as *Papyrus*. Sister boat to above.
Etoile Du Nil I (63 plus 2 suites), built 1990, refurbished 2004.
CATARACT NILE CRUISES www.cataractint.com
Hotel and cruise boat operator.
Princess Amira (67)
La Reine Du Nil (68)
Sobek (48)
CREATIVE HOTELS AND RESORTS www.worldofcreative.com
Nephtis (55 plus 4 suites), former Hilton International boat.
Shehrayar (38 plus 2 suites)
Shehrazad (38 plus 2 suites)
Ti-Yi (63)
Tu-Ya (63)

DYNASTY FLOATING HOTELS www.nile-vision.com
Nile Vision (56)
EASTMAR TRAVEL www.eastmar-travel.com
Older company.
Ra I (72), built in Yorkshire.
Ra II (73), UK-built.
Atlas (41, ****), 4 decks.
Nile Star (30 plus 3 single, ****)
EGYPTIAN CANADIAN NILE CRUISES www.montasser investment.com
Montasser I (80)
Montasser II
Stephanie (78), refurbished 2007. Mixed reviews from UK passengers.
Miss Universe (59, ***)
EL ESTEKLAL EL GEDIDA www.emiliotravel.com
Also run the Emilio Hotel in Luxor.
Domina Prestige (62 plus 8 single and 2 suites), light, open; piano bar.
ESADORA NILE CRUISES Tel: 02-2418 1219
Miss Esadora (68), tinted blue windows.
Royal Esadora (61)
ETAPES NOUVELLES EGYPTE VOYAGE www.etapes-eg.com
Part of a large French group.
Beau Rivage I (73), built 2001, entrance like an Egyptian temple.
Beau Rivage II (75), built 2005.
Voyageur (74), built 1994, renovated 2002.
EXTENSION GROUP www.extensiongroup.com.eg
Founded 1997.
Concerto (63 plus 4 suites), newest of the fleet and classed NN.
Miss World (66 plus 4 suites)
Mozart (65)
Princess Sarah (66 plus 4 suites)
FLASH NILE CRUISE www.flashtour.com
Established 1985; also run Red Sea resorts with strong Italian links.

Cheops (68 plus 4 suites), also known as *Arabesque*.
Lady Mary (72), also called *Magic Lady Mary*.
Lady Carol (68 plus 4 suites), also called *Magic Lady Carol*.
Magic I (72)
Magic II (72), new sushi bar.
Royal Club (20), also known as *Lady Karin*, with split-level sundeck.
Karim Palace (34 plus 2 suites, ****), 4 decks. Renovated 2004.
Juliana Palace (34 plus 2 suites, ****), 4 decks, sister boat to *Karim Palace*.
Reve Du Nile (48, **), older boat.
FLOPATTER NILE CRUISES Tel: 02-2450 2327, email: beausoleil@menanet.net.
Beau Soleil (74), gaudy pink and blue paintwork.
FLORENCE SAINT MARIA www.florencesaintmaria.com
Florence (76)
GLORY NILE CRUISE Tel: 02-2633 1316
Glory (55)
FLOTEL NILE CRUISES Tel: 02-2737 5055
Nile Beauty (79)
Nile Romance (80)
GRAND CIRCLE HAPI NILE CRUISES www.gct.com
Part of Grand Circle Tours, who operate river cruises worldwide.
River Anuket (70), launched 2001.
GRAND FOR NILE TOURISM www.redseahotels.com
Boats operate under the name Grand Cruises, www.grand-cruises.com.
Grand Rose (60 plus 2 suites)
Grand Palm (63 plus 2 suites)
Grand Preziosa (52 plus 2 suites)
Grand Sun (60 plus 2 suites)
Grand Glory (49 plus 1 suite)
Grand Star (62 plus 2 suites)
Nile Beauty (46), 4 decks.
Nile Romance (70)

Suntimes (60 plus 2 suites)
HAPI TRAVEL & TOURISM Tel: 02-2393 3562
Hapi 5 (71)
Queen Of Hanza (75)
Hapi 2 (33, ***)
HASSAN SHALKAMY GROUP CRUISES www.shalkamy-eg.com
Egyptian Princess (61), built 1985.
El Fostate (81 suites), built 2002.
King Tut I (81 suites), also known as *Queen of Escape*, built 2003.
King Tut II (81 suites), built 1998.
King Tut III (81 suites), built 1999.
King Tut IV (81 suites), built 2004.
Ramses of Egypt I (37), smaller boat of 3 decks and split sundeck.
Ramses of Egypt III (84 suites), built 1989.
Nile Hadeer (36, ****), built 1979.
King Tut Fleet (45, ***), built 1980.
INTER.CO. FOR NILE CRUISING Tel: 02-2735 4228
Egilkia (65)
INTER NILE CRUISES
Armada (80)
Serenade (67)
INTER TEAM NILE FESTIVAL www.interteam.com.eg
Nile Festival (64)
ISIS NILE CRUISES AND HOTELS www.isistravel.com
Well-established company begun in 1933.
Nile Crown I (58)
Nile Crown II (63)
Nile Crown III (63), also known as *M/S Tag El Nil*.
Queen Isis (43 plus 3 single), smaller boat.
Coral I (70, ****), 4 decks.
Coral II (68 plus 2 suites, ****), 4 decks.
Ninfea I (34, ****)
Telestar I (57, ***)

ITALIAN EXPRESS NILE CRUISES www.niledolphin.com
Nile Dolphin (65)
ITALIAN EXPRESS TOURIST SERVICES www.italianexpresscruises.com
Nile Jewel (54), 4 decks plus half sundeck.
JJW HOTELS & RESORTS www.jjwhotels.com
Operate two sister ships under the name *Amarante Nile Cruises*, details at www.amarantenilecruises.com.
Amarante Isis (37 suites)
Amarante Osiris (37 suites)
JOLLEYS TRAVEL & TOURS www.jolleys.com
Alexander the Great (30 suites), www.alexanderyacht.com.
L'AUBE VOYAGE www.laubevoyage.com
L'Aube Du Nile (68)
LILAC HOTELS INTERNATIONAL www.lilachotels.com
Operating as *Elegant Voyage*, www.elegantvoyage.com.
Kon-Tiki (64 plus 6 suites)
Moondance (58 plus 8 suites)
Sindbad (32 plus 2 single plus 2 suites, ****), 4 decks.
MASTERS TRAVEL SERVICE www.mtsegypt.com
Alyssa (72), www.alyssanilecruise.com.
MEMNON NILE CRUISES www.memnontours.net
Nile Smart (74 plus 2 suites), 4 decks, built 1989.
Nile Smile (74 plus 2 suites), built 1988.
Nile Supreme (74 plus 6 suites), built 1993.
Nile Elite (74 plus 6 suites, ****), built 1992.
Also *Nile Marquis* and *Nile Zeina* (part of Song of Egypt, *see page* 132).
MIROTEL FOR FLOATING HOTELS www.tarottours.com
Formed 1979, also run the Azur Hotels chain.
Champollion II (43 plus 7 suites)
Fleurette (46 plus 2 suites)
Leonardo da Vinci (62, 2 single and 4 suites), also known as *Da Vinci*.
Nile Azur (55 plus 2 single and 5 suites)

Star of Luxor (52 plus 2 suites), split-level sundeck.
Sun Azur (36 plus 2 suites, ****), 4 decks, also known as *El Tarek*.
Tarot (62 plus 4 suites)
Also offer the *Oberoi Zahra (see page 130).*

MISR INTERNATIONAL NILE CRUISE Tel: 02-2633 1316
Preziosa (50)

MOEVENPICK HOTELS & RESORTS www.moevenpick radamis.com
Swiss luxury all the way.
Radamis I (61 plus 4 suites)
Radamis II (69 plus 6 suites)

NAGGAR TRAVEL AGENCY www.naggartravel.com
Founded 1961 and owner of Nabila Nile Cruise Fleet (with 'Queen Nabila Fleet' often written on the side of each boat).
Al Nabilitan (65), built 1999.
King of Thebes (70)
Queen of Sheeba (78)
Ramses King of the Nile (65)

NILE CO. FOR HOTELS & NILE CRUISING Tel: 02-2735 0676
Cheops III (70), slightly older. Red and white decor.

NILE CRUISES www.solaris2-eg.com
Solaris I (61 plus 5 suites), also known as *Nile Caesar*.
Solaris 2 (67 plus 3 single)

NILE EXPLORATION www.nile-exploration.com
Three identical sister boats:
Royal Orchid (24 cabins plus 4 suites)
Royal Rhapsody (24 cabins plus 4 suites)
Royal Serenade (24 cabins plus 4 suites)
Plus two boats managed by Moevenpick Hotels & Resorts:
Royal Lily (56 plus 4 suites), www.moevenpick-royal-lily.com.
Royal Lotus (60 plus 2 suites), www.moevenpick-royal-lotus.com.

NILE SUN CRUISES www.nilesun.com
Nile Ruby (74 suites)

Royal Ruby (66 plus 2 single and 1 suite)
OBEROI INVESTMENT LTD www.oberoihotels.com
Two of the most luxurious cruise boats on the Nile.
Oberoi Zahra (27 luxury cabins and suites), classed NN.
Oberoi Philae (50 plus 4 single and 4 suites), each cabin with its own private balcony.
OPTIMA CRUISES www.optimacruises.com
Amarco I (45 plus 4 suites and 4 cabins for guests with disabilities), renovated 2008.
NATIONAL TRAVEL SERVICE www.ntsegypt.com
Grand Princess (68 suites)
Miss Egypt (68 suites), covered in reflective glass.
Royal Princess (62 suites)
NILE BRIDE CRUISES www.nilebridestory.com
Nile Bride (70)
Nile Story (68)
PALM INVESTMENT FOR HOTELS Tel: 02-2633 1316
Palm I (72)
PARTNER COMPANY Tel: 02-3761 2478
Partner Hotp (54)
Partner Tut (54)
PHOENIX FOR INVESTMENTS Tel: 02-2415 3331
La Dolce Vita (83), usually Blu Club.
PRESIDENTIAL NILE CRUISES www.pnccruises.com
Established 1979; at the forefront of developing Nile cruising.
Nile Admiral (85)
Nile Commodore (76)
Nile Legend (73)
Nile Odyssey (73)
Nile Plaza (84), 4 decks.
Nile Ritz (79)
Nile Symphony (84)
PYRAMIDS NILE CRUISES

Adonis (71)
PYRAMISA HOTELS & RESORTS www.pyramisaegypt.com
Pyramisa 2 Amr Courd (83)
Pyramisa Champollion I (51)
Pyramisa Champollion II (51)
Pyramisa Napoleon (72)
Pyramisa Nile Angel (47)
Pyramisa Vitto Rai (67)
QUEEN TOURS EGYPT www.queentours-eg.com
Also called *Queen Nile Cruises.*
Nile Pioneer I (62 plus 2 suites), built 1999.
Nile Pioneer II (64 plus 2 suites), built 2005.
Nile Pioneer III (64 plus 2 suites), built 2010.
ROWAD TOURISM Tel: 02-2735 5297
River Pioneers II (72)
SABENA HOTELS & CRUISES www.sabenagroup.com
Al Jamila (66 plus 4 suites)
Al Kahila (68 plus 4 suites)
Farida (55)
SAKKARA TRAVEL GROUP www.sakkaragroup.com
Lady Diana (71 suites), built 1989, renovated 2009.
Zen Mojito (70 suites), built 2005.
Zen Monaco (68), built 2003.
Zen Monte Carlo (73 suites), built 2002.
Zen Nile Dream (45, ****), built 1983, renovated 1999.
SELECTION FOR HOTELS & NILE CRUISES www.selectiongroup.net
Formed 1995. These sister boats are two of the oldest on the Nile, both refurbished in 2004.
Anni (13 plus 2 single and 37 suites)
Aton (13 plus 2 single and 37 suites)
SETI FIRST TRAVEL www.setifirst.com
Company started in 1978; also owns the Seti Hotel at Abu Simbel.

Allegra Emerald (34 plus 1 suite)
Allegra Platinum (68 plus 2 suites)
Astra (68), renovated 2010.
Castello Diamond (4 plus 36 suites), 4 decks.
Castello Grand Diamond I / II / III (10 suites on each boat), new breed of luxury cruisers with huge suites and top class personal service.
Castello Ruby (46 plus 2 suites), wonderful glass-domed lobby.
Rocco Gold (59 plus 6 suites)
Rocco Silver (74, ****)
Excelsior (63)
Alessandra (72, ****)
Le Pascha (35, ****)
SHALAKANI TOURS Tel: 02-2517 2080
Oonas (40)
OonaS II (46, ****)
SHAMS NILE FOR FLOATING HOTELS Tel: 02-2417 0046
Nile Shams (74)
SHERRY NILE CRUISES www.sherryboat.com
Sherry Boat (61 plus 2 suites)
SILVER MOON NILE CRUISES www.moonrivertours.com
Moon River (55)
Silver Moon (38, ****)
SONESTA INTERNATIONAL www.sonestacruises.com
Operated by Sakkara Travel Group, www.sakkaragroup.com.
Sonesta Moon Goddess (50 suites), built to a high standard in 2000.
Sonesta Sun Goddess (62 suites), built in 1993, renovated in 2002.
Sonesta Nile Goddess (47 plus 6 suites), renovated in 2009.
Sonesta Star Goddess (33 suites), built 2006.
Sonesta St George I (47 plus 10 suites), luxury all the way on one of the newest boats on the Nile.
SONG OF EGYPT www.songofegypt.net
Marquis II (62 plus 2 suites)
Nile Marquis (65 plus 4 suites)

Opera (86 plus 15 suites), longer and larger boat.
Zeina (68 plus 4 single and 2 suites)
SOUTH SINAI NILE CRUISES www.miragecruise.com
Mirage I (60 plus 2 suites), sleek, with narrow windows.
SPHINX TOURS & NILE CRUISES www.sphinxtours.com
Citadelle (60 suites)
Golden Queen (35), 4 decks, also known as *Nile Queen*.
SPRING TOURS www.springtours.com
Carmen (46), built 2003, refurbished 2007.
Giselle (58 plus 2 suites)
Karim (15), 4 decks. Beautifully restored 1917 rear-wheeled paddle steamer previously used by kings and presidents of Egypt.
La Boheme (40), built 2008.
La Traviata (43 plus 2 single), recently renovated.
Media (56 plus 2 single and 2 suites)
Miriam (56 plus 2 single and 2 suites)
Nile Sapphire (69 plus 2 single), renovated in 2009.
Nile Secret (55), renovated 2010.
Norma (56 plus 2 single and 2 suites), built 1997, refurbished 2006.
Salome (36), renovated 2010.
Tosca (41 suites), one of the most lavish, modern boats on the river.
Pensee (53, **)
SUNRISE RESORTS & CRUISES – EGYPT www.sunrisehotels-egypt.com
Newer company (2003), operating cruise boats and Red Sea resorts.
Semiramis I and *II* (66 plus 4 suites), identical sister ships.
Semiramis III (64 plus 2 suites), built 2007.
Terramar (20 suites), 4 decks. Smaller boat.
TIVOLI FOR TOURISM INVESTMENT Tel: 02-2450 9615
Nile Style (81)
TOWER NILE CRUISE COMPANY Tel: 02-2414 5630
Tower I (73)
TRANS EGYPT TRAVEL www.transegypttravel.com

Salacia (31 suites), re-fitted 2006 with large suites.
Triton (21 suites), large suites.

TRAVCOTELS www.travcotels.com

Travco are one of the largest tour operators in Egypt. They own and operate the largest number of Nile cruise boats.

Iberotel Crown Empress (128), largest boat in their fleet at 110m (361ft) in length.
Iberotel Crown Emperor (120), second largest at 100m (328ft).
Chateau Lafayette (55)
Crown Jewel (80)
Crown Jubilee (80), also known as *Jaz Jubilee.*
Crown Prince (80)
Crown Regent (80), also known as *Regent*, usually Club Magic Life.
Helio (50), slightly older style of 4 decks and split-level sundeck.
Imperial (50), cabins are larger than average, usually Club Med.
Jaz Senator (17 VIP suites only), smaller luxury boat with 4 decks.
Jaz Legacy (72 plus 2 singles and 2 suites), new boat.
Jaz Minerva (77), new boat.
Lady Sophia (70), through Italian operator Alpitour.
Lady Christina (74)
Le Lotus, specialises in day cruises to Dendera and dinner cruises.
Nile Empress (29), 4 decks and split-level sundeck.
Nile Monarch (45), 4 decks and split-level sundeck.
Regency (52), also known as *Jaz Regency*.
Regina (60)
Royale (52), also known as *Jaz Royale*.
Nile Pearl (23, ***)
Nile Sovereign (32, ***)

TRAVEL WAYS EGYPT www.travelways-egypt.com

Nile Carnival (72), launched 1999 with sleek blackened windows.
Nile Crocodile (57), also known as *Crocodilo*. Refurbished 2003.

TRAVELINE EGYPT www.traveline-eg.com

Formed 2002, representing several British tour operators.

Darakum (44 plus 8 suites), larger luxurious vessel, built 2008.
Hamees (72), built 2001.
Misr (14 plus 2 singles and 8 suites), restored royal steamship initially built in Preston in 1918 and used by King Farouk.
Sunray (62 plus 2 suites)
TURQUISE FOR FLOATING HOTELS Tel: 02-3335 1807
Kasr El Nil (50, ****)
UNITED NILE CRUISE COMPANY www.mssoleil.com
Soleil (30 plus 2 single and 2 suites), 4 decks
VIKING NILE CRUISES www.viking-egypt.com
Royal Viking (68 plus 4 suites), built 2009.
Viking Princess (52 plus 4 suites), refurbished 2009.
WINGS TOURS & NILE CRUISES www.wingsegypt.com
Jasmin (62), split level sundeck. Launched 1988, modernised 2001.
Orchid (58 plus 4 suites), launched 1989, refurbished 2000.
Tamr Henna (66), most modern of the Wings fleet.
Tulip (40 plus 16 suites)
WISDOM TOURS www.nilequest.com
Founded 2000, dealing mainly with Spanish and American groups.
Nile Quest (66), also known as *Al Andalus*.
ZAMALEK NILE CRUISE Tel: 02-2735 7726
Prince Omar (73)

OTHER CRUISE BOATS

Four-star rated. Of note is the four-star *Sudan* (18 plus 5 suites, www.steam-ship-sudan.com). This paddle steamer was built in 1885, restored in 2000 and featured in the TV version of *Death On The Nile*.

In addition to those already indicated above, there are several other four star boats: *Ambassador II* (42), *Evergreen* (40), *Granada* (40), *Hatshepsut* (36), *Horizon* (105), *Horus* (45), *King Mina* (56), *Nile Splendour* (78), *Orchestra* (68), *Renaissance* (76), *River Pioneers I* (66), *Rosetta* (48), *Royal Regency* (70), *Salima* (45), *Telestar II* (51), *Userhat* (47), *Viking Premiere* (58).

Three-star rated. *African Queen* (54), *Ahmos* (44), *Aida III* (91), *Gondola* (25), *Monaliza* (33, also known as *Monalisa*), *Nile Majesty II* (88), *Prince De La Vie* (25), *River Hathour* (15), *Verdi.*
Two-star rated. *Cinderella* (22), *Doma III* (24, 3 decks plus sundeck).

LAKE NASSER CRUISE BOAT OPERATORS

Thanks to the wide open space of Lake Nasser, some of these vessels are larger than regular Nile cruise boats. All are rated five stars with consistently good luxury facilities and service.

BELLE EPOQUE TRAVEL
Eugenie (52 plus 2 suites), www.eugenie.com.eg. Built in 1993, this was the first boat to open up Lake Nasser to the public.
Kasr Ibrim (55 plus 10 suites), www.kasribrim.com.eg. Built 1997, designed and fitted in classic 1920s Art Deco style.

HIGH DAM CRUISES www.highdamcruise.com
Nubian Sea (66 plus 4 suites), launched 1995.

LAKE NASSER ADVENTURES www.lakenasseradventures.com
Two small boats and a cruiser for small adventure groups or families.
Nubiana (4), cabin cruiser built 2007.
Ganoub and *Bahr El-Nouba*, safari boats with sleeping area.

MOEVENPICK HOTELS & RESORTS
Prince Abbas (43 plus 22 suites), www.moevenpick-prince-abbas.com. Modern boat built along the classic lines of an old steamer.

NAGGAR TRAVEL AGENCY www.naggartravel.com
Queen of Abu Simbel (76)

SUNRISE RESORTS & CRUISES (EGYPT) www.sunrisehotelsegypt.com
African Dreams (87 cabins and suites), each of its five decks is decorated in different African themes.

TRAVCOTELS www.travcotels.com
Jaz Omar El Khayam (80), ultra-modern large boat at 107m (351ft) in length, 17m (56ft) in width and 2.5m (8ft) draft.
Tania (28), three decks and split-level sun deck.

DAHABIYA OPERATORS

Named after their golden paintwork (*dahab* means gold), these classic two-masted sailing boats were used by Victorian travellers. With the arrival of paddle steamers, they fell out of favour through the 20th century and most were scrapped or rotted away. However, a few were saved and recently put into service to provide a luxuriously nostalgic base from which to explore the antiquities. So successful have they become as private charters that new versions are being built complete with a/c, Wi-fi and all mod cons. They operate special itineraries between Luxor and Qena, Esna and Aswan rather than a set weekly timetable. Overnight stops are possible where larger cruise boats cannot moor, such as Gebel Silsila. Large operators are beginning to discover this tranquil and more personal style of Nile cruising, together with many single vessel owners/operators.

Not all of the older boats have a/c, so check, and they might need to be towed by a motor launch if there is no wind. Newly built *dahabiyas* have their own engines. Prices are not cheap, but the facility to hire the entire boat make these craft unique. A *sandal* is a large converted *felucca*, also with twin masts and usually three cabins.

AFRICAN ANGLER www.african-angler.net
Miran (6)
CREATIVE HOTELS and RESORTS www.worldofcreative.com
Operate four new sister dahabiyas:
Om Kolthoum
Eva Peron
Agatha Christie
Grace Kelly
DAHABIEH www.dahabieh.net
Nile Heaven II (8 plus 2 suites), sleeps 20 passengers. Lots of good sailing information on the website.
DIDIER CAILLE www.dahabeya.net
Vivant Denon (2 plus 2 single), maximum 6 guests on this boat,

over 100 years old. Only available for a few weeks per year, no a/c.
NILE SAILING www.nilesailing.com
Cenderella (4 plus 1 suite)
Africa (6 plus 2 suites)
They also offer two converted sandals:
Kareem (3)
Bab Il Nil (3)
NOUR EL NIL www.nourelnil.com
Often moored at Esna. Panoramic suites on each boat are marvellous.
Assouan (6 plus 2 suites)
El Nil (8 plus 2 suites)
Malouka (6 plus 2 suites)
Meroe (8 plus 2 suites)
NUBIAN NILE CRUISES www.nubiannilecruises.com
El Bey (6)
El Hanem (6)
Nesma (6)
Zahra (6)
Also have a converted *sandal*, *Royal Cleopatra* (3)
RIVER EGYPT www.riveregypt.net
Giraffa (10), built in 1840, has been completely revamped.
Rehab (3), is a smaller, family-sized converted sandal, built in 1906.
SPRING TOURS www.springtours.com
Amoura (6 plus 1 suite), constructed 2008 with large sundeck.
Judi (8 plus 1 suite), constructed 2008.
SETI FIRST TRAVEL www.setifirst.com
Gawaher, constructed 2010.
Ghawayesh, constructed 2010.
SONESTA INTERNATIONAL www.sonestacruises.com
Amirat (6 plus 2 suites), constructed 2009.
TRAVCOTELS www.travcotels.com
Elite Dahabiya (8), modern sailboat offering top class facilities.
Prestige Dahabiya (8), starts cruising in 2011.

Recommended Hotels

Adding a few days to your trip at the start or finish of your cruise will usually be at a hotel in Luxor. Most hotels are located in the tourist district, along Shari' Khaled Ibn Al Walid between the Iberotel and Sheraton Hotel. Both Luxor and Aswan are surprisingly small considering the numbers of tourists. Peak rates are in the winter, especially over Christmas and towards Easter. Amazing deals can be had at every standard of hotel through the hot, quiet summer season. As a basic guide, prices are for a standard double room for one night, including taxes and breakfast, during peak season.

££££	over £65
£££	£25–65
££	£10–25
£	under £10

LUXOR

Al Moudira £££–££££ *Daba'iyya, West Bank (12km/7½ miles south of the ticket office via Memnon Colossi); tel: 012-325 1307; www.moudira.com.* The Al Moudira looks like a Moorish palace-meets-hammam. Beautifully laid out around a central courtyard-garden, the rooms are individually and attentively furnished. There's an extensive garden, a serene pool and a reputable restaurant *(see page 103)*, but it's the tranquillity and service that really make it stand out.

Amoun Al Gazila £ *Gezirct Al Bairat, West Bank (near the ferry landing, left at the Mobil petrol station); tel: 095-231 0912.* The building is nothing special, but the setting amid sugar-cane fields, the views over the Theban hills, the verdant garden and the fantastic home cooking make this family-run place really special. Rooms are simple but clean, and rates depend on facilities (some have private bathrooms).

Beit Sabée ££ *Near Madinat Habu Temple, Kom Lolah, West Bank; tel: 010-632 4926; email: info@nourelnil.com.* The Beit Sabée is a beguiling mud-brick house with simple but tasteful rooms done out in local palettes, textiles and furnishings. With just eight rooms, it's stylish but intimate and homey.

Marsam Hotel £ *Opposite Valley of the Nobles, West Bank; tel: 095-2372 403; www.luxor-westbank.com/marsam_e_az.htm.* The West Bank's original hotel, built close to the major site of Luxor, the delightful domed mud-brick Marsam offers 30 very simple but clean rooms around a courtyard, with good home cooking to boot.

New Emilio Hotel ££ *Shari' Yousef Hassan, East Bank; tel: 095-237 3570; emilio_hotel@hotmail.com.* Ever-popular for its comfortable rooms equipped with satellite TV, fridge, telephone and air-con, as well as a business centre, sauna, small pool and sun deck on the roof, the Emilio represents Luxor's best mid-range option.

Philippe Hotel £££ *Shari' Dr Labib Habashy, East Bank; tel: 095-238 0050; fax: 095-238 0050.* The Philippe offers spotless air-conditioned rooms with television and fridge, some with balconies, plus roof terrace, small pool and bar. Book well ahead.

Sofitel Old Winter Palace ££££ *Corniche An Nil, East Bank; tel: 095-238 0425.* One of Egypt's most historic hotels, this is a national institution. Victorian-palatial in design, it also boasts luscious formal gardens, a gorgeous pool, tennis courts and some first-class restaurants. Rooms are spacious and comfortable; many have views over the Nile. Historic, romantic, comfortable and well run, it's worth a splurge.

Sonesta St George Hotel £££–££££ *Shari' Khaled Ibn Al Walid, East Bank; tel: 095-238 2575; www. sonesta.com/egypt_luxor.* It's not the most handsome building, but the St George offers great amenities and rooms at good prices. Rooms are well furnished and spacious (some have Nile views), and there's a large pool with sun deck and bar, outdoor jacuzzis, a gym and two good restaurants *(see page 104)*.

ASWAN

Beyt el-Kerem £ *North of the Tombs of the Nobles, West Bank; tel: 019-2399 443 ; www.experiencenubia.com.* This modern house has an attractive roof terrace, lovely views and good home cooking. Rooms (with shared bathroom) are very simple but clean, and the hotel is welcoming and peaceful. A good range of activities, including fishing, painting and Nile swimming, can be organised. To get here, take the ferry opposite the railway station to the West Bank. It's then a five-minute walk north along the river.

Isis Hotel £££ *Corniche An Nil, East Bank; tel: 097-231 7400; www.pyramisaegypt.com.* The Isis has comfortable chalet-style rooms set in a garden with a pool and a couple of restaurants serving European cuisine. It is also centrally located right next to the Nile.

Keylany Hotel ££ *25 Shari' Keylany, East Bank; tel: 097- 232 3134; www.keylanyhotel.com.* Offering simple, clean and well-furnished rooms with air-conditioning, satellite television and private bathrooms, the Keylany is Aswan's best budget bet. The management is efficient and helpful, and there's a pleasant roof terrace for drinks, a small pool and spa, plus an in-house internet café.

Mövenpick Resort Aswan ££££ *Elephantine Island; tel: 097-230 3455; www.moevenpick-aswan.com.* Despite an unattractive exterior, this is one of Aswan's best places to stay. Recently renovated, the luxury spa hotel occupies the northern tip of the island and has its own ferry service. Facilities include a garden, pool and good spa facilities.

Sofitel Old Cataract Hotel ££££ *Shari' Abtal At Tahrir; tel: 097-231 6000; www.sofitel.com.* This is arguably the Nile's most iconic and historic hotel. Agatha Christie is said to have partly written *Death on the Nile* here (it also served as the set of the movie). Due to reopen in May 2011, this Moorish-meets-modern hotel will comprise deluxe suites, a vast terrace, a huge spa and a wellness centre. *See page 105.*

ABU SIMBEL

Seti Abu Simbel ££££ *On Lake Nasser; tel: 097-340 0720; www.setifirst.com.* Abu Simbel's only five-star hotel has chalet-style rooms set in a garden fronting Lake Nasser. Comfortable, well equipped and tranquil, though a little overpriced.

INDEX

Berlitz pocket guide

Nile Cruising

First Edition 2011

Written by Chris Bradley
Series Editor: Tom Stainer

Photography credits
All Pictures APA/Glyn Genin except:
Alamy 4BL, 96
Chris Bradley 21, 22, 29, 42, 76, 82, 88, 89, 98/99
ENTA/Bertrand Reiger 2TR, 54
Flop Eared Mule 3TR
Dennis Jarvis 53

Cover picture: 4Corners Images

Printed in China by CTPS

Contact us

At Berlitz we strive to keep our guides as accurate and up to date as possible, but if you find anything that has changed, or if you have any suggestions on ways to improve this guide, then we would be delighted to hear from you.

Berlitz Publishing, PO Box 7910,
London SE1 1WE, England.
fax: (44) 20 7403 0290
email: berlitz@apaguide.co.uk
www.berlitzpublishing.com